Thomas Kelly Cheyme

The Book of Psalms

Thomas Kelly Cheyme
The Book of Psalms
ISBN/EAN: 9783744774642
Printed in Europe, USA, Canada, Australia, Japan
Cover: Foto ©Lupo / pixelio.de

More available books at **www.hansebooks.com**

THE
BOOK OF PSALMS

TRANSLATED BY THE

Rev. T. K. CHEYNE, M.A.

NEW YORK
D. APPLETON AND COMPANY
1, 3, AND 5 BOND STREET
MDCCCLXXXIV

INTRODUCTION.

I.

THE best Introduction to the Psalter is the practice of free and unconstrained private devotion. A bad translation of an uncorrected text will be more illuminative to a devout mind than the choicest and most scholarly rendering to an unsympathetic reader. The Psalter stands alone as a devotional classic of the first rank in virtue of its originality, and only he who is to some extent original in his religious life, and who waits upon the Giver of all good things for impulses and inspirations, can appreciate the freedom and vigour of the expressions and ideas of the Psalms. It is not just to these precious lyrics, however, to read them exclusively in a version several centuries old. Exquisite as the Prayer-book version may be, and possibly the Bible version too to ears unfamiliar with the older music, either rendering does but convey that part of the meaning and the charm which was accessible to the men of the sixteenth century. The rhythmic effect of the old versions of the Bible (on which Mr. Matthew Arnold, in *Isaiah of Jerusalem*, lays so much stress) may be admirable of its kind, but it is not the lightning-like effect of the Hebrew ; the collocations of words and syllables may be suggestive, but they are often miles removed from the sense of the original ; and loose as may be the connection of thought in an Eastern lyric, it is not so loose as the connection in our Prayer-book and Bible versions. It is therefore not unjustifiable to offer a new translation of the Psalms, which, though its diction has not been uncared for, does not pretend to give a faithful echo of the rhythms of the past.

There is no irreverence in this; Hebrew scholars can be catholic in their literary tastes, and if they lay it down as a canon of translation, that sense should generally take precedence of sound, it is not because they are deaf to the charm of rhythmic melody. Nor ought they, at this hour of the day, to be accused of temerity in deviating from the received Hebrew text. The younger school of Hebrew scholars looks upon the textual and exegetical tradition much as the Sanskrit school represented by Mr. Max Müller looks upon the exegetical tradition of Sayana, and earnestly as it deprecates the excesses of some isolated critics, will not pretend to translate that which cannot be translated, simply because the frequent irregularities of Hebrew usage make some current rendering, apart from exegesis, not absolutely inadmissible. The present translator is very conscious of his fallibility ; but he prefers to offer in such cases a plausible and worthy rendering, based upon some natural emendation, to airing his grammatical acumen at the expense of propriety and connection. Rather than do this, indeed, he has sometimes left a blank in his version to indicate that the text is perhaps corrupt, and certainly to the translator unintelligible.

INTRODUCTION.

It need hardly be said that he has profited by good suggestions wherever he has found them; Dr. Kay's translation may be mentioned in particular as a most helpful and scholarly version of the received text. Keble's too little known metrical version has now and again supplied a felicitous phrase; it is the production of a poetical student, though as a work of art it cannot compare with the metrical German translation, or rather reproduction, of the Psalms by one of the most studious of poets, Julius Hammer. Another metrical version, also in German, arrived too late to be of use. Its author, Dr. Gustav Bickell, had, however, already published a metrical edition in Hebrew of the poetical parts of the Old Testament, which, though too bold to be adopted as a basis in its entirety, proved an invaluable supplement to the already existing text-critical apparatus. The author of the famous article, "Israel," in the *Encyclopædia Britannica* (Julius Wellhausen), has well remarked that, whatever may be said of Dr. Bickell's supposed metrical discoveries, his critical labours have often led him to self-evident corrections of the Hebrew text.

The object of the present edition is to enable lovers of literature to read the Psalter intelligently and with pleasure. The Dictionary of the Bible and the various commentaries on the Psalms will supply the *student* with learned material in abundance. But the ambition of the publishers and the translator is to make the Psalms enjoyable, and learned controversies are not æsthetically enjoyable. A few points, however, require to be mentioned here in order to promote an intelligent pleasure in these lyrics. The first, which is one of the fruits of the Semitic renaissance due to Assyriology and Egyptology, is that the Psalms are not so entirely exceptional as many of us have believed. Even in Israel, indeed, the tone of thought and feeling characteristic of the Psalms was much more widely spread than a one-sided study of the Old Testament might lead us to suppose. The proper names preserved in the Hebrew records prove this; and when we discover that the Hebrew proper names may be paralleled by those of Assyria, we are prepared to find it not too bold an assertion, that it was only the want of the higher spiritual prophecy as a teaching and purifying agent, and of a longer course of development, which prevented the sacred poetry of Babylonia and Assyria from rivalling that of the successors of David. Let me quote one or two passages to prove that, however short their flights, the Babylonian poets were no strangers to the regions of spiritual devotion.

1 The anger of my lord's heart,
   may it be appeased!
2 O god, may the ignorant come unto wisdom!
   O goddess, may the ignorant come unto wisdom!
3 The god who knows what is unknown,
   may he be appeased!
4 The goddess who knows what is unknown,
   may she be appeased!

5 I am cast down,
   and none reaches forth his hand to me.
6 I weep in silence,
   and no man takes my hand.
7 I utter my prayer,
   and none hears me.
8 I am enfeebled, overwhelmed,
   and no man delivers me.

9 O my god, my sins are seven times seven,
   absolve my sins

10 O my goddess, my sins are seven times seven,
   absolve my sins!
11 God, who knowest what is unknown,
   my sins are seven times seven, absolve my sins!
12 Goddess, who knowest what is unknown,
   my sins are seven times seven, absolve my sins!

13 Absolve my faults!
   guide thou him who submits himself to thee!
14 May thy heart, as the heart of a mother who has brought
   forth, be appeased!
15 As the heart of a mother who has brought forth, and of a
   father who has begotten,
   may it be appeased![1]

Making every allowance for the obscurity of the language, and the consequent uncertainty of some phrases in the translation, this is certainly a remarkable production for "a date anterior to the 17th century B.C."[2] Now take another, which, like the foregoing, is preserved in an Accadian or proto-Babylonian and in an Assyrian form. The moon-god, Sin, is addressed.[3]

1 In the heaven who is exalted?
   Thou. Thy commandment is exalted.
2 Upon the earth who is exalted?
   Thou. Thy commandment is exalted.
3 Thy will, even thine, is published in the heaven,
   and the archangels of heaven bow down their faces.
4 Thy will, even thine, is published on the earth,
   and the archangels of earth kiss the ground.
5 Thy will, even thine, from above, like the space of heaven in
   its openness,
   makes the earth to bring forth.

[1] Lenormant, "The Penitential Psalms of the Chaldeans." *The Academy*, July 20, 1878.
[2] Sayce, *Records of the Past*, vol. vii. p. 151.
[3] Lenormant, *Études accadiennes*, t. ii. p. 147.

6 Thy will, even thine, makes contracts and justice to exist,
  establishing contracts for men.
7 Thy will is it, even thine; in the distant heavens and the
  vast earth
  thou spreadest happiness, and bearest no grudge to any.
8 Thy will, even thine, who knows it?
  who could change it?
9 O Lord, in the heaven is thy lordship; in the earth is thy
  sway;
  among the gods thy brethren thou hast no rival.

I have quoted psalms of Accadian origin, because the Accadian religious poets stood to the Assyrians and later Babylonians in much the same relation as the Hebrew psalmists to the Christian hymn-writers. It may be an extravagance to suppose, with the author of *Hebrew Mythology*, that the similarity between the sacred poetry of the Israelites and that of their neighbours is due to the influence of the latter upon the former during the Babylonian Exile, but it is clear that if we reject this hypothesis we must admit that the "Spirit of holiness" was attracting and educating suitable scholars on the banks of the Euphrates and the Tigris as well as on those of the Jordan.

I might now proceed to institute a comparison of portions of the Egyptian with the Hebrew psalmody, but forbear. Two or three fine passages have been quoted in the notes, and Egyptian religion has not the elementary affinities with the Israelitish which are possessed by that of Mesopotamia. I might also bring out at length the darker side of the Babylonian religious poetry, but this would conduce to a misconception of the true state of things. It is the germs of higher religious poetry that we find in the Babylonian, and not more. We have hardly a better right to compare the Babylonian sacred poetry as a whole with the Hebrew, than the Vedic. In common language the Hebrews were much more "fortunately placed" than the authors of the Babylonian and of the Sanskrit Vedic hymns. Of Dean Church's thoughtful comparison between the latter and the Hebrew psalms, Mr. Max Müller has well said that it is only from a Christian point of view that we can prefer the Psalms. To a historical mind, there can be no question of preference. "It is *because* the Veda" (and the Babylonians too had their Veda) "places before us a language more primitive than any we knew before; it is *because* its poetry is what you call savage, uncouth, stupid, horrible, it is for that very reason that it was worth while to dig and dig till the old buried city was discovered, showing us what man was, what we were, before we had reached the level of David, of Homer, of Zoroaster."[1]

II.

"The level of David;" the words are soon spoken, but how difficult it would be to prove them in a literal or superficial sense! In fact, the name, when used in connection with the Psalms, is but a symbol for a certain bold originality of style combined with a deeply devotional spirit. If there are any psalms which do not exhibit these signs, they are not Davidic, whatever the titles may say, which, in most cases, indeed, a little common sense will dissolve into thin air. The question whether any of the psalms can be Davidic is variously answered. A reasonable respect for tradition would incline us to reply affirma-

[1] *Transactions of the Oriental Congress*, 1876, pp. 202-3 (Address to the Aryan section).

matively. The contrast between the David of the historical books and the David even of the eighteenth Psalm is certainly strong, but, as Carlyle has reminded us, " What are faults—what are the outward details of a life, if the inner secret of it—the remorse—temptations—the often-baffled, never-ended struggle of it be forgotten?"[1] Whether the answer is sufficient will depend in no small measure on the course which we attribute to Israel's religious development; whether, in short, we take Ewald or Kuenen for our master. Happily the beautiful elegy upon Saul and Jonathan (2 Sam. i. 19-27) has never had its Davidic origin questioned; but this is not more religious than the banqueting songs of David alluded to in Am. vi. 5. The little fragment at the end of Psalm xxiv. (ver. 7-10) is also, if not Davidic, at least of very ancient origin.

It is at any rate a great relief to realize that only a very small number of psalms can reasonably be ascribed to David, and that of those which remain a large proportion are written either (like the complaints of Job) in the name of a representative righteous man, or of the pious Israel personified. "The Psalms," says the great preacher Adolphe Monod, " are all filled with expressions of an unheard-of sorrow. David there speaks incessantly of his troubles, of his maladies, of his innumerable enemies; as we read them, we can hardly understand what he meant."[2] Most true; it passes human understanding. But when we remember the fondness of Eastern races for personification, and the striking examples of the figure as applied to Israel or Jerusalem to be found elsewhere both in phraseology

[1] *Heroes and Hero-worship*, p. 219.
[2] *Les Adieux d'Adolphe Monod*, p. 83.

(*e.g.* in the phrase "the daughter of Zion," Isa. i. 8, Mic. iv. 10), and in connected passages (*e.g.* in the first and third of the Lamentations, in some of the so-called Psalms of Solomon,[1] in certain parts of 2 Isaiah, and in the striking monologue of the true Israel in Mic. vii.), we are naturally inclined to apply this key to the seemingly hyperbolical expressions of so many of the Psalms. The explanatory notes in this edition will show some of the happy results of the application.

The so-called imprecatory psalms, in particular, gain when looked at from this point of view. As long as they are interpreted of an individual Israelite, they seem sadly inconsistent with the benevolent spirit of the finest parts of the Old Testament. If, however, they are spoken in the name of the nation, or at any rate of those with the most awakened consciences, the strong figures and intense feeling become intelligible. The words of Coleridge are still more applicable to these psalms on what we may call the national theory. "In the fierce and inordinate I am made to know and be grateful for the clearer and purer radiance which shines on a Christian's paths, whilst in the self-oblivion of the heroes of the Old Testament, their elevation above all low and individual interests,—above all, in the entire and vehement devotion of their total being to the service of their divine Master, I find a lesson of humility, a ground of humility, a ground of humiliation, and a shaming yet rousing example of faith and fealty."[2]

Further, not only is a large proportion of the psalms congregational in the strictest sense, but the book itself

---

[1] I mention these two books first as containing religious lyrics. On the Psalms of Solomon, see below.
[2] *Confessions of an Inquiring Spirit*, p. 35.

as a whole comes to us with the authority of the Synagogue as a Book of Common Prayer and Praise. First of all, however, it appears to have passed through several editions. How much, it may be asked, was included in the first edition?

To answer this question with some degree of probability, I must first of all point out that the Psalter appears to be made up of several smaller collections. A superficial glance at the Psalter is enough to prove this. Take for instance—

I. Psalms iii.-xxxii., xxxiv.-xli. All these are inscribed as Davidic, except Ps. x., which is properly the second part of Ps. ix. This forms one collection.

II. Psalms xlii.-lxxii. Of the psalms in this collection, xlii.-l. are ascribed to the sons of Korah (a family or guild of temple-singers), li.-lxxii. to David himself (with the exception of lxvi., lxxvii., and lxxi. which are anonymous, and lxxii., which is given to Solomon).

The chief reason for separating collections I. and II. (apart from the doxologies at the end of Psalms xli. and lxxii.) is the peculiar preference of the name Jehovah to Elohim in the former, and of Elohim to Jehovah in the latter. One of the strangest phenomena in the Psalter is the existence of duplicate versions of Psalms xiv. and xl. 13–17 (see Psalms liii., lxx.). There are, it is true, several other variations of text in them, but the most striking peculiarity is that we find Jehovah six times changed to Elohim, and the converse of this only once. It can hardly be doubted that a later editor, for some reason or other, scrupled at the frequent use of the name Jehovah:

INTRODUCTION.

either he reverenced it too much, or he feared seeming to imply that the true God was the God of the Jews alone. It should be added that the third collection agrees in its preference of Elohim with the second, and according to some was really its other half, the second collection consisting properly of Davidic psalms alone. In this case Psalms xlii.-l. have been misplaced, and belong properly to the beginning of the next collection.

And yet, though separate in their origin, it is plausible to hold that these two collections were joined together as they stand, with the addition of Psalms i., ii., and xxxiii. to make up the favourite number seventy, thus forming the first comprehensive psalm-book. This must have taken place after the Exile, for even these two first collections contain a number of psalms of the Exile: two psalms indeed belong to the Maccabean period (xliv., lx.), but these were doubtless inserted subsequently to the provisional completion of the Psalter.

III. Psalms lxxiii.-lxxxix. These were all written for liturgical purposes. At least, they are all ascribed to the temple-singers, except Ps. lxxxvi. ("a prayer of David"), and Ps. lxxxix., which is referred to Ethan the Ezrahite. Psalms lxxiii.-lxxxiii. are ascribed to Asaph; Psalms lxxxiv.-lxxxviii. to the sons of Korah. This was evidently the next contribution to the psalm-book, which, like its predecessor, appears to have received some additions in the time of the Maccabees, e.g., Psalms lxxiv., lxxix., and perhaps lxxv., lxxvi., lxxx., lxxxiii., lxxxix.

The latter part of the book is rather more loosely arranged. Psalm xc., with its meditative complaint on the lapse of time, seems to have been placed first out of regard to the contents of Ps. lxxxix. (*comp*. ver. 47 of this psalm). The groups of psalms which can still be traced are (*a*) Ps. xciii., xcv.-c., and (*b*) Ps. cxi.-cxviii., which are connected respectively by the similarity of their contents, also (*c*) Ps. cxx.-cxxxiv., each inscribed "a song of the upgoings (of the pilgrims to Jerusalem)," and (*d*) Ps. cxlvi.-cl., all of which are Hallelujah psalms for the congregation. Ps. cl., as the reader will see, is as suitable for the conclusion of the Psalter as Ps. i. is for the Introduction.

Out of these various small groups, with the addition of some isolated psalms, the fourth of the larger collections was formed, in all likelihood, not much before the compilation of the Chronicles. The psalm ascribed to David in 1 Chron. xvi., 7-36, on the removal of the ark to Jerusalem, is but a cento of passages taken from it.[1] Here too there are probably some Maccabean psalms, *e.g.*, at any rate, cxviii. and cxlix. Finally, the last of the editors of the Psalter divided the fourth collection at the end of Psalm cvi.,[2] perhaps to make the Psalter correspond externally to the venerated "Books of Moses." This was not done unadvisedly. In the eyes of this pious scribe, the Psalter was the answer of the worshipping community to the demands made by its Lord in the Law, the reflection of the external standard of faith and obedience in the utterance of the believing heart. To those who tell us that post-Exile Judaism was a lifeless fossil, our reply is, look at the post-Exile psalms, especially the cxixth.

[1] Verses 8-22 are taken from Ps. cv. 1-15 ; verses 23-33 from Ps. xcvi. 1-13; verses 34, 35, from Ps. cvi. 1, 47.

[2] He did this by taking over a verse, very awkwardly, from 1 Chron. xvi. 36, as a doxology.

If the poetical value of these is less than that of the earlier psalms, the quality of the religious life expressed in them is surely finer and more spiritual. With all their love for the Law, it is not the ritual forms which they honour most, but "the weightier matters," which the later Pharisees so sadly forgot. In fact, it was by no means the Law alone that they studied. There is internal evidence enough that some of the prophets, especially Jeremiah and "the Second Isaiah," afforded them constant food for thought, and hence it is that the Exile and post-Exile psalms present us with a synthesis in varying proportions of the legal and the prophetic religion. Concentration on the Law (but not as a mere system of rites), may be the characteristic of a few (*e.g.* Ps. i., xix. 1-7, xl., cxix.), but an all-absorbing love to God is the soul of a much larger number. That purer conception of the Deity, which chilled the author of Ecclesiastes almost into infidelity, became to the psalmists a fresh source of light and warmth (*see* Psalms cxiii., cxlvi., cxlvii.). The more they assimilated it by loving meditation, the more replete they found it with important results for the religious life. It is these later psalms, in fact, which almost justify the saying, that "the spiritual side of Christianity is inherited from the Hebrew psalmists." Original they may not often be, but passages really striking in their simplicity abound. Thus in Ps. lxxxvi. we find the most distinct of the Old Testament prophecies of the conversion of all nations (ver. 9). What a sweet humility, moreover, breathes in the phrase, "Save the son of thy handmaid" (ver. 16), and what an earnest belief in Providence in the petition, "Work in my behalf a token for good" (ver. 17,—*comp.* Neh. v. 19). And lastly, three at least of the psalms of this period (ciii., civ., cxxxix.) are not unworthy to be classed among the gems of the Psalter.

III.

The Psalter, like our modern hymn-books, contains poems of very different ages, its range, perhaps, extending over 500 years. The translator has renounced the idea of even a tentative chronological arrangement, while fully recognizing the suggestive utility of that adopted from Ewald by the "Four Friends." Still, wherever the comprehension of a psalm seemed especially to depend on an approximation to the date, he has not refrained from giving one; and he would have the reader always bear in mind that grand principle, for enunciating which a grateful homage is due to the memory of Herder, that every psalm has a back ground of historical circumstance, and must be somewhat vague and obscure until this is discerned—an application, in fact, of Goethe's well-known dictum that all good poems are called forth by an occasion (*Gelegenheitsgedichte*).

It is hardly necessary, except for the sake of completeness, to justify the form of parallel lines in which the psalms are printed. The student of the Old Testament, who only knows the ordinary editions, has no means of distinguishing poetry from prose. He may, indeed, when better instructed, retort upon the critics that by their own confession the poetical parts of the Old Testament have few indeed of what are called the forms of poetry,—no metre, only a slight tendency to rhyme, and a strong affection for alliteration. Perhaps it may be so, although a succession of critics (among them, quite lately, Dr. Bickell, of whom mention has been made already) deny that Hebrew poetry is entirely destitute of metre. But at any rate the deficiencies referred to are partly compensated for by the elaborateness of the rhythm. "Hebrew poetry," as I have said elsewhere, "is the poetry of emotion, and emotion, like the sea, expresses itself, not in the onward rush of a single gigantic breaker, but in the rise and fall of a succession of waves;" or, to speak without figure, each verse of a Hebrew lyric, and the same was apparently the rule in Accadian psalmody, consists of a couplet, a double couplet, or a triplet, embodying a more or less complete parallelism of expression and of thought.[1] Such, at least, is the rule, the theory, the ideal, though practice does not always ratify the precept. Even in the psalms, and much more in the prophecies, we often meet with a simple bifurcation of a verse, without either complete or incomplete parallelism. In fact, too constant an adherence to the rule would be wearisome, especially in prophetic oratory. The latest examples of sustained parallelism are the so-called Psalms of Solomon, eighteen in number, written probably in Hebrew, but

---

[1] For specimens of this parallelism take the following:—

Synonymous, incomplete.	Mine eyes languish towards the heavens; Jehovah, I am hard pressed, be surety for me.—Is. xxxviii. 14.
Synonymous, complete.	What ails thee, O thou sea, that thou fleest? And thou Jordan that thou turnest back? Ps. cxiv. 5.
Antithetic.	Faithful are the wounds of a friend, And plentiful the kisses of an enemy. Prov. xxvii. 6.
Progressive, *i.e.* containing repetition with a climax.	The torrent of Kishon swept them away, The onward-rushing torrent, the torrent of Kishon.—Judges v. 21.

now only extant in a Greek form. They appear to have been finished after the murder of Pompeius, B.C. 48, and represent the last known efflorescence of the religious lyric poetry of the Jews previous to the destruction of the temple. It would probably have been hopeless at that late date to have attempted to introduce fresh psalms into the sacred collection.

IV.

But if the Psalms of Solomon were excluded by their modern origin, there must have been other lyrics fully adequate to any test, and yet refused admittance among the Psalms of David. Some of them are enshrined in other parts of the Old Testament, and will be read with as much enjoyment as the songs of the Psalter. Here are a few specimens.

1. THE SONG OF MOSES (Ex. xv. 1-18).

1 I will sing to Jehovah, for he was majestic ;
   the horse and his rider he cast into the sea.
2 Jehovah is my strength and my song,
   for he became salvation to me:
   such is my God, and I will beautify him,
   my father's Dread, and I will exalt him.

3 Jehovah, a man of war, Jehovah is his name;
4 Pharaoh's chariots and host he threw into the sea,
   and his best chariot-warriors were drowned in the Sea of Reeds.
5 The floods covered them over,
   they went down into the abysses like a stone.

6 Thy right hand, Jehovah, that art glorious through might,
   thy right hand, Jehovah, dashed in pieces the enemy.

INTRODUCTION.   xxi

7 And in the greatness of thy majesty didst thou pull down thine
   assailants,
   thou sentest forth thy hot wrath which devoured them as
   stubble,
   and by the breath of thy nostrils the waters were piled up.

8 The streams stood up like a heap (of corn),
   the floods stiffened in the heart of the sea.
9 The enemy said, I will pursue,
   I will overtake, I will divide spoil;
   my desire shall be filled with them;
   I will draw my sword, my hand shall exterminate them.

10 Thou didst blow with thy wind, the sea covered them,
   they sank as lead in the glorious waters.
11 Who is like thee among the gods, Jehovah,
   who like thee is glorious in holiness?
12 Terrible in famous deeds, worker of wonders,
   thou stretchedst forth thy right hand, the earth swallowed
   them.

13 Thou didst lead in thy lovingkindness
   the people that thou hadst released;
   thou didst gently lead them by thy strength
   to thy holy habitation.
14 The peoples heard it, they trembled;
   pangs took hold of the dwellers in Philistia.

15 Then were confounded the chiliarchs of Edom,
   Moab's bell-wethers, quaking took hold of them;
   all the dwellers in Canaan melted away,
   dread with shuddering fell upon them.
16 By the greatness of thine arm they became still as a stone,
   until thy people, Jehovah, pass over,
   until the people that thou hast gotten pass over.

17 Thou broughtest them and plantedst them
   in the mountain of thine inheritance,
   [where] thou hast prepared thee a place to dwell in,
   (and) thy hands, O Lord, have established a sanctuary.
18 Jehovah shall be king for ever and for ever.

In ver. 2, for *Dread* (Heb. *elōhīm*), comp. Milton's "our living Dread in Silo his bright sanctuary," and Max Müller's *Science of Religion*, ed. 1, pp. 179-180.

Clearly this song was not intended for the place it now occupies. For it refers not only to the overthrow of Pharaoh but to the conquest of Canaan by Joshua ; and as Canaan was only won by slow degrees, it would almost appear that the song cannot have been written till long after the Israelites were settled. However this may be, the style, which is peculiar, does not favour a very late date. Ewald thinks that a really ancient song was filled out and added to by the historian.

2. THANKSGIVING-PSALM OF HEZEKIAH

(Isa. xxxviii. 10-20).

10 I said, "In the noontide of my days must I depart—
    into Hades gates, amerced in the rest of my years."
11 I said, "I shall see Jah no more in the land of the living,
    nor look at men with dwellers in the world."
12 My habitation is plucked up,
    and carried away from me like a shepherd's tent ;
    thou hast cut off like a weaver my life ;
    between day and night thou wilt make an end of me.
13 I cried out for help until the morning,
    (as a lion did he break all my bones :)
    "between day and night wilt thou make an end of me"?
14 Like a swift or a crane did I scream ;
    I moaned as a dove, mine eyes longed heavenwards ;
    Jehovah, be careful for me, become my surety.

15 What can I say? he both spake and hath kept his promise !
    I shall walk at ease all my years despite my soul's bitterness.
16 O Lord ! *   *   *   *
    and thou wilt recover me and make me to live.

INTRODUCTION.

17 Behold, for my welfare came this bitterness unto me,
and thou hast kept my soul from the pit of destruction;
for all my sins hast thou cast behind thy back.
18 For Hades cannot thank thee, Death cannot praise thee;
those who have gone down to the grave cannot hope for thy truth:
19 The living, the living, he shall thank thee, as I do this day;
the father to the children shall make known thy truth.
20 Jehovah is for my deliverance,
and my stringed instruments will we strike
all the days of our life in Jehovah's house.

The song expresses the feelings of King Hezekiah during his illness and after his wonderful recovery, but was not unfit for any pious Israelite who had had providential experiences. It is full of reminiscences of Job and the Psalms, but is a sweet, plaintive specimen of the more artificial kind of Hebrew psalmody. It may be doubted whether, like the preceding psalm, it was not written a good while later than the event referred to. The text seems to be in parts incorrect; ver. 16 in particular challenges the ingenuity of the interpreter.

3. THE FIRST OF THE LAMENTATIONS OF JEREMIAH.

1 How does she sit in solitude—the city that was full of people!
she is become a widow that was great among the nations!
the princess among the provinces, she is become a vassal!
2 She weeps sore in the night, and her tears are on her cheek;
comforter has she none out of all those that loved her:
all her friends have betrayed her, they are now her enemies.
3 Judah is become an exile for affliction and for much travail;
she has sat down among the nations, but has found no place of rest;
all her pursuers have overtaken her amidst her straits.

4 Mournful are Zion's roads for lack of festal pilgrims,
    all her gates are waste, full of sighs her priests;
    her virgins led in train, herself in bitterness.
5 Her foes are now the head, prosperous her enemies,
    Jehovah having grieved her for her multiplied transgressions;
    her children are gone away, captives before the foe.
6 And from the daughter of Zion vanished is all her splendour,
    her princes are become like harts that have found no pasture,
    and they take their weary way before him that pursued.
7 Jerusalem bears in mind her affliction and persecution,
    when her people were the prize of the foe, and she had none to help her;
    how the foes beheld her, and laughed that she was extinguished.
8 Deeply did Jerusalem sin, therefore was she an abomination,
    all that once honoured her vilified her, for they saw her nakedness:
    she herself was full of sighs, and turned backward.
9 Her impurity was on her skirts—she had not thought upon her future,
    so that she came down wondrously, she had none to comfort her:
    "behold mine affliction, Jehovah, for proudly deals the enemy."
10 The foe stretched out his hand upon all her precious things;
    yea, she saw heathen men who had entered into her sanctuary,
    of whom thou gavest commandment that they should not grieve thee by entering.
11 All her people have been sighing, seeking for bread,
    they have given their precious things for food, to refresh the soul,
    "behold, Jehovah, and look, how I am lightly esteemed."
12 "Ho, all that pass by the way, look ye and see,
    if there be a pain like mine, the pain which was given me,
    with which Jehovah grieved me, in the day of the burning of his anger.
13 From high heaven he sent fire into my bones, and made it to prevail;
    he spread a net for my feet, backward did he turn me;
    he made me stunned and faint all the day long.

14 The yoke of my transgressions is bound, by his hand they are twined together;
   they are come up upon my neck, he has made my strength to fail;
   the Lord has given me into hands which I have not power to resist.
15 All my strong ones within me the Lord lightly regarded;
   he proclaimed a festival against me to crush my young warriors:
   the Lord trod the wine-press for the virgin-daughter of Zion.
16 For these things am I weeping, mine eye runs down in water,
   for no comforter is near, who might refresh my soul;
   my children are desolate, for the enemy was too strong."
17 Zion stretches out her hands, none has she to comfort her;
   Jehovah appointed unto Jacob those around him to be his foes;
   an abomination among them became Jerusalem.
18 "Righteous is Jehovah, for his mouth did I defy;
   hear now, all ye peoples, and behold my pain:
   my virgins and ripe young men are gone into captivity.
19 I called unto my lovers, but they cast down my hope,
   my priests and ancient men breathed their last in the city,
   when they would fain get food that they might refresh their soul.
20 Behold, Jehovah, for I am in straits; mine inward parts seethe:
   my heart turns round within me, because I was so defiant:
   without the sword bereaveth, within as it were the plague.
21 They have heard how I sigh, with none to comfort me;
   all mine enemies have heard, they rejoice that thou hast done it:
   bring the day thou hast proclaimed, that they may be like me.
22 Let all their wickedness come before thee, and do unto them—
   according as thou didst unto me for all my transgressions!
   for many are my sighs, and my heart is faint."

Jeremiah's authorship of the Lamentations is defended by few modern critics, but none will deny that they express the ideas of the spiritual children of that great prophet. Apart from its own peculiar beauties, the elegy translated above has an additional illustrative value, since parts of it are spoken by one of the current personifications of the pious portion of the people of Israel. The third Lamentation would have been still more valuable in this respect, but it is much longer and æsthetically is less attractive. The style of composition is no doubt artificial, the elegy selected being a perfect example of the alphabetic psalm (comp. note on Psalm ix., p. 218). Such poetry was in favour with the exiles, not so much from "the sad mechanic exercise—Like dull narcotics, dulling pain," as because of the welcome aid which it afforded to the memory. The Lamentations (which are included by Ewald in his translation of the Psalms) were in fact evidently intended for congregational use on one of the fast-days, though we have no positive evidence that they were so employed till after the destruction of the second temple. In later times, the fast-days called a multitude of elegies into existence, in which the feelings of the nation towards Zion personified are pathetically expressed, as even lovers of the most modern literature know through Heinrich Heine. Not "the songs of ambrosial Homer" would this gifted prodigal son of Israel enshrine in the famous casket of Alexander, but

"the Zion-song
which Jehuda ben Halevy
dying on the sacred ruins
of Jerusalem indited."

But let us return to the point from which we started. To appreciate either the dying song of Jehuda Halevy, or the far nobler sources of his inspiration, is impossible simply from the point of view of æsthetic criticism or comparative national psychology. They are more than lyric poems; more than monuments of the strongest known patriotism; they are classical expressions of a faith in the unseen which dominated the lives of the poets, and only grew deeper as the shades of midnight fell.

POSTSCRIPT.

The translator has often enough envied Chaucer's command of English, but can at least fully appropriate the modesty of his "envois." Only the greatness of the need would have justified the present attempt. Were the Psalms to be represented in the *Parchment Library* by a mere adaptation of a version intended (like Coverdale's) for the unlettered people and not for lovers of poetry? And yet how attempt a task which a critic like Mr. Matthew Arnold has told us that he declines? How venture on a kind of translation of the Bible hitherto reserved for scholars alone, and use such "unbiblical" words as "sympathy" and "æon"? Possibly indeed some literary readers may think that the one is sufficiently authorized by Milton and the other by Tennyson. But what of "loving" as applied to Jehovah and his worshippers? Scholars may very plausibly criticise it, but what other rendering is not too cold and pale to express the peculiar Hebrew conception of the religious sentiment? But is not "Hades" an anachronism? Not more so in an English than in a Greek version; not more so than "hell," and not nearly so misleading. Will any one seriously propose Sheól as a substitute in a literary version? At any rate, "the earthborn," "mortal man," "deadly shade," imply antiquated scholarship and desertion of Ewald? Is it certain? Are not many other false etymologies sanctioned by the Hebrew writers? But the reader who seeks to enjoy his Psalms will cry out if I parley any longer with the critics. I will only assure him again that he cannot climb up to David's Psalms by Coverdale's ladder, and that I well know that my own or any version of a masterpiece like the Psalter can be only partially successful.

As in the case of the Revised Version of the New Testament, which I neither praise nor blame for its English, some of my renderings will be accused of wilfulness, simply because I have here and there followed a corrected text. I have referred to this already, and will only mention a very few of the passages in which the meaning, as it seems to me, has gained by a justifiable emendation, generally at the suggestion of Olshausen, Lagarde, or Bickell: viii. 1; x. 6, 14; xvi. 2, 3; xviii. 29; xx. 5; xxii. 30, 31; xxiv. 6; xxix. 6, 7; xxxi. 11; xxxv. 13; xxxvi. 1; xlv. 6; xlviii. 2; xlix. 7, 11; lviii. 9; lx. 4; lxviii. 9, 18, 30; lxix. 4, 10, 26; lxxii. 16; lxxvi. 4; lxxxiv. 5; lxxxv. 13; lxxxviii. 15; cii. 7; cix. 10; cx. 3; cxxxvii. 5; cxl. 10.

⁎ The symbol ᵉ at the head of some psalms (thus VIIᵉ.) means that the translation of the psalm referred to involves one or more emendations; words inclosed in square brackets represent Hebrew words supposed to have dropped out of the text.

THE PSALMS.

BOOK I.

PSALM I.

HAPPY the man that has not walked in the counsel of the ungodly,
    nor stood in the way of sinners,
    nor sat in the company of scoffers!
2 But in the law of Jehovah is his delight,
    and on his law meditates he day and night.
3 For he is like a tree planted by water-courses,
    that brings forth its fruit in due season,
    and whose leaf withers not;
    and whatever he does, makes he to prosper.

4 Not so are the ungodly,
    but they are like the chaff which the wind drives away.
5 Therefore the ungodly cannot stand in the judgment,
    nor sinners in the assembly of the righteous.
6 For Jehovah favours the way of the righteous,
    but the way of the ungodly perishes.

II. Wherefore do the nations throng together,
   and the peoples meditate vanity?
2 The kings of the earth stand forth,
   and the rulers take counsel together,
   against Jehovah and against his anointed:
3 "Let us tear off their bonds," (say they),
   "and cast from us their cords."

4 He who is seated in the heavens laughs,
   the Lord mocks at them.
5 Then speaks he unto them in his anger,
   and in his hot wrath confounds them:
6 ". . . When *I* have established my king
   upon Zion my holy mountain."

The King speaks.

7 "I will relate a decree:
   Jehovah said unto me, Thou art my son,
   I have this day begotten thee.
8 Ask of me, and I will grant thee
   nations for thine inheritance,
   and the earth's utmost parts for thy possession.
9 Thou shalt break them with a mace of iron;
   thou shalt shiver them like a potter's vessel."

10 Now therefore, ye kings, deal wisely;
   be admonished, ye judges of the earth.
11 Serve Jehovah with fear,
   and testify awe with trembling.

12 Kiss the Son,
> lest he be angry, and ye go to ruin,
> for his anger kindles easily:
> happy all those that take refuge in him!

III. JEHOVAH, how many are my foes become!
> many are they that rise up against me.
2 Many are saying of my soul,
> "there is no salvation for him in God".

3 But thou, Jehovah, art a shield about me,
> my glory, and the lifter up of my head.
4 I cry aloud unto Jehovah,
> and he answers me from his holy mount.

5 I laid me down and slept,
> I have awaked, for Jehovah sustains me.
6 I am not afraid of the myriads of people
> that have arrayed themselves against me round about.

7 Arise, Jehovah; save me, O my God!
> for thou smitest all mine enemies upon the cheek-bone,
> thou breakest the teeth of the ungodly.
8 Salvation is Jehovah's;
> thy blessing be upon thy people!

IV. ANSWER me when I call, O God of my righteousness!
> when I was in straits thou didst set me at large;
> have pity upon me, and hear my prayer.

2 O sons of men, how long shall my worship be disgraced,
   because ye love vanity, and seek after falsehood?
3 But see how passing great kindness Jehovah hath shown me;
   Jehovah hears when I call unto him.

4 Tremble, and sin no more:
   consider in your heart upon your bed, and be still.
5 Offer the right sacrifices,
   and put your trust in Jehovah.

6 Many are saying, O for the sight of good fortune!
   Jehovah, lift thou up the light of thy countenance upon us.
7 Thou hast put more joy into my heart
   than when others have their corn and new wine in abundance.
8 In peace will I at once lay me down and sleep,
   for thou, Jehovah, makest me dwell alone in safety.

V. GIVE ear unto my words, Jehovah,
     understand my murmuring.
2 Listen to the sound of my crying, my King and my God,
   for unto thee will I make my prayer.
3 Jehovah, in the morning shalt thou hear my voice;
   in the morning will I order (my sacrifice) for thee,
     and will look out.

4 For thou art not a God that has pleasure in wickedness,
   evil cannot be a guest of thine:

5 Boasters cannot stand up before thine eyes,
   thou hatest all them that work naughtiness:
6 Thou wilt destroy them that speak lies;
   the man of blood and of deceit Jehovah abhors.

7 But I, because of thine abundant kindness, can enter thy house,
   can worship toward thy holy palace in the fear of thee.
8 Jehovah, lead me in thy righteousness, because of mine adversaries;
   make thy way level before my face.
9 For there is no sincerity in their mouth,
   their inward part is very destruction;
   an open grave is their throat,
   their tongue do they make smooth.

10 Declare them guilty, O God,
   let them fall by their own plots;
   for the multitude of their transgressions thrust them down,
   for they have rebelled against thee:
11 And let all that take refuge in thee be glad,
   and ring out their joy for ever;
   and O protect them, that they may triumph in thee
   who love thy name.
12 For thou, Jehovah, givest thy blessing to the righteous;
   with favour, as with a buckler, surroundest thou him.

VI. JEHOVAH, do not in thine anger reprove me,
neither in thy wrath correct me.
2 Have pity upon me, Jehovah, for I am languishing;
heal me, Jehovah, for my bones are confounded.
3 My soul also is confounded exceedingly;
but thou, Jehovah, how long?

4 Return, Jehovah, deliver my soul,
save me, for thy lovingkindness' sake.
5 For in Death there is no mention of thee,
in Hades who will give thee thanks?
6 I am wearied with my groaning,
every night make I my bed to swim,
I melt away my couch with my tears.
7 Mine eye has fallen in from vexation,
it has grown old by reason of all my foes.

8 Away from me, all ye that work naughtiness,
for Jehovah has heard my loud weeping.
9 Jehovah has heard my supplication,
Jehovah will receive my prayer.
10 Ashamed and sore confounded be all mine enemies,
let them turn back with shame suddenly!

VIIe. JEHOVAH my God, in thee have I taken refuge;
save me from all my pursuers, and deliver me:
2 Lest he tear my soul as a lion,
when there is none to rescue, and none to deliver.

3 Jehovah my God, if I have done this,
   if there be iniquity in my hands,
4 If I have wrought evil unto him that was at peace with me,
   or oppressed him that was my foe for nothing,
5 Let the enemy pursue my soul, and overtake it,
   yea, let him trample my life to the earth,
   and lay my glory in the dust.

6 Arise, Jehovah, in thine anger,
   lift up thyself against the fury of my foes,
   yea, rouse thyself toward me—a sentence hast thou commanded:
7 And let the assemblage of the peoples come about thee,
   and return thou over it unto the high heaven.
8 Jehovah judges the peoples;
   right me, O Jehovah, according to my innocence
   and to the integrity pertaining unto me.

9 O that the wickedness of the ungodly might come to an end,
   and that thou wouldest establish the innocent,
   thou trier of the hearts and reins, thou righteous God!
10 My shield over me is God,
   the saviour of the upright in heart.

11 God is a righteous judge,
   and a God who threatens angrily every day.
12 If any will not turn, he will whet his sword;
   he has bent his bow and made it ready,
13 And has aimed at the man the weapons of death,
   setting his arrows aflame.

14 Behold, he travails with naughtiness;
   he both conceives mischief and brings forth a lie.
15 A pit has he dug and hollowed it out,
   and he will tumble into the (very) pitfall he made.
16 His mischief shall return upon his own head,
   upon the crown of his own head shall his violence descend.
17 I will thank Jehovah according to his righteousness,
   and make melody unto the name of Jehovah most high.

VIIIe. JEHOVAH our Lord,
   how glorious is thy name in all the earth!
whose majesty is exalted above the heavens.
2 With the mouth of children and sucklings hast thou founded a stronghold
   because of thy foes,
   to still the enemy and the revengeful.

3 When I behold thy heavens, the work of thy fingers,
   the moon and the stars, which thou didst establish,
4 What is mortal man, that thou art mindful of him,
   and the son of the earth-born, that thou visitest him?
5 For thou madest him little less than divine,
   and didst crown him with glory and worship;
6 And thou hast made him to rule over the works of thy hands,
   all things hast thou put under his feet,
7 Sheep and oxen, all of them,
   moreover the beasts of the plain,

8 The fowl of the heaven, and the fish of the sea,
    that which traverses the paths of the seas.
9 Jehovah our Lord,
    how glorious is thy name in all the earth!

IXe. I WILL thank Jehovah with my whole heart;
    I will tell out all thy wonders.
2 I will be glad and triumph in thee,
    I will make melody to thy name, O Most High!

3 Because mine enemies turn backward,
    stumble and perish at thy presence:
4 For thou hast maintained my right and my cause,
    thou art seated on the throne, judging righteously.

5 Thou hast rebuked the nations, destroyed the ungodly,
    their name hast thou wiped out for ever and ever.
6 The enemies are consumed, they are perpetual ruins:
    and the cities which thou didst uproot—the memory of them has perished.

7 *They* may perish, but Jehovah shall be seated for ever;
    he has prepared his throne for judgment:
8 And he shall judge the world in righteousness,
    he shall give doom to the peoples in equity:

9 That Jehovah may be a sure retreat for the downtrodden,
    a sure retreat for times of hopeless trouble;

10 And that they who know thy name may trust in thee,
 since thou, Jehovah, dost not forsake those that inquire after thee.

11 Make melody unto Jehovah, whose seat is in Zion,
 publish his exploits among the peoples,
12 How that he who requires blood has been mindful of them,
 he has not forgotten the cry of the afflicted,—

13 "Have pity upon me, Jehovah; behold my affliction from them that hate me,
 thou that liftest me up from the gates of Death:
14 That I may tell out all thy praise in the gates of the daughter of Zion,
 that I may exult in thy salvation."

15 The nations are sunk in the pit that they made,
 in the net which they hid is their foot taken:
16 Jehovah has made himself known, he has executed judgment,
 snaring the wicked in the work of his own hands.

17 The ungodly shall depart to Hades,
 all the nations that are forgetful of God.
18 For the needy shall not alway be forgotten,
 the expectation of the afflicted shall not perish for ever.

19 Arise, Jehovah, let not mortal man be too strong;
 let the nations be judged in thy presence.
20 Strike them with terror, Jehovah;
 let the nations know that they are mortal men.

X⁣e. **W**HY, Jehovah, standest thou afar off,
 and coverest (thy face) in times of hopeless trouble?
2 Proudly doth the wicked persecute the afflicted:
 they are caught in the knaveries which those have devised.

3 *   *   *   *   *   *
    *   *   *   *   *   *

4 The wicked, in his arrogance . . . "He will not punish,"
 "there is no God," is the sum of his thoughts.

5 His ways are stable at all times.;
 thy judgments are too high in heaven for him to see,
 as for all his foes, he puffs at them.

6 He has said in his heart, "I cannot be moved;
 I shall never bow down for all generations."
7 His mouth is full of cursing, deceits, and oppression,
 under his tongue are mischief and trouble.

8 He sits in the lurking-places of the villages,
 in hiding-places he slays the innocent:
 his eyes are on the watch against the hapless.

9 He lurks in a hiding-place as a lion in his lair,
 he lurks to catch the poor;
 he catches the poor, dragging him with his net.

10 * * * and, being crushed, (the poor) sinks down,
   and the hapless fall by his strong ones.
11 He has said in his heart, "God has forgotten,
   he has hidden his face, he can never see it."

12 Arise, Jehovah! O God, lift up thy hand,
   forget not the afflicted.
13 Wherefore does the wicked contemn God,
   saying in his heart, "Thou wilt not punish?"

14 Thou hast seen it; for thou lookest on mischief and vexation,
   to shew forth [vengeance] with thy hand;
   to thee the hapless commits his all—
   thou showest thyself the helper of the orphan.

15 Break thou the arm of the wicked,
   and the evil man's wickedness—punish it, till thou find none.
16 Jehovah is King for ever and ever:
   the heathen are perished from his land.

17 Jehovah, thou hast heard the desire of the afflicted,
   thou establishedst their heart, thou madest attentive thine ear,
18 To right the orphan and the down-trodden,
   that mortals of the earth may overawe no more.

XIe. IN Jehovah have I taken refuge; how say ye to my soul,
   "flee to your mountain, ye birds?

2 For lo! the ungodly bend the bow,
   they make ready their arrow upon the string,
   to shoot unseen at the upright in heart.
3 When the foundations are being cast down,
   what can the righteous do?"

4 Jehovah is in his holy palace,
   Jehovah's throne is in heaven;
   his eyes behold, his eyelids try the children of men.
5 Jehovah approves the righteous,
   but the ungodly and him that loves violence his soul hates.
6 Upon the ungodly he shall rain coals, fire and brimstone,
   and a burning wind shall be the portion in their cup.
7 For Jehovah is righteous, he loves righteous acts,
   the upright shall behold his countenance.

XIIe. SAVE, Jehovah, for the man of love is no more,
   for the faithful have vanished from among the children of men.
2 They speak falsehood every one with his neighbour:
   with flattering speech and with a double heart do they speak.

3 May Jehovah cut off all flattering lips,
   and the tongue that talks grandly,
4 Those that say, "With our tongue do we make a firm covenant,
   our lips are our allies; who is lord over us?'

5 For the oppression of the afflicted, for the groaning
of the needy,
 now will I arise, saith Jehovah,
 I will set him in the safety for which he pants.
6 The words of Jehovah are pure words,
 silver smelted * * *,
 seven times refined.

8 All around, the ungodly walk to and fro,
   *   *   *   *   *   *
7 Thou, Jehovah, shalt keep us,
 and shalt guard us from this generation for ever.

XIIIe. How long, Jehovah, wilt thou forget me for ever?
 how long wilt thou hide thy face from me?
2 How long shall I lay up sorrow in my soul,
 with heaviness in my heart day and night?
 how long shall mine enemy exalt himself over me?

3 Look hither and answer me, Jehovah my God,
 lighten mine eyes, lest I sleep unto death;
4 Lest mine enemy say, "I have prevailed against him,"
 and my foes exult because I am moved.

5 But as for me, in thy loving kindness is my trust;
 let my heart exult in thy salvation.
6 Let me sing unto Jehovah, for he has dealt bountifully with me.

XIVe. THE fool says in his heart,
"there is no God."
Corrupt and abominable are their practices,
there is none that does good.

2 Jehovah looked down from heaven
upon the children of men,
to see if there were any that dealt wisely,
and inquired after God.

3 It has all turned aside, all alike have become tainted;
there is none that does good.

*   *   *   *

no, not one.

4 Shall they not rue it, all that work naughtiness,
that eat up my people?
They have eaten up the bread [of the afflicted],
they have not called upon Jehovah.

5 Thereupon shall they shudder indeed, for God
is in the righteous generation.
6 Ye would frustrate the purpose of the afflicted!
yea, but Jehovah is his refuge.

7 Oh that the salvation of Israel were come out of
Zion!
when Jehovah turns the fortune of his people,
let Jacob exult, let Israel be glad.

XV. JEHOVAH, who shall be a guest in thy pavilion?
who shall dwell upon thy holy mountain?
2 He that walks blamelessly, and works righteousness,
and speaks truth in his heart:
3 He that has no slander upon his tongue,
that does no ill to his companion,
nor utters a reproach against his neighbour:
4 In whose eyes a reprobate is contemned,
but those that fear Jehovah doth he honour;
if he swear to his hurt, he changes not:
5 He that gives not his money for usury,
nor takes a bribe against the innocent:
he that does these things shall never be moved.

XVIe. PRESERVE me, O God; for I seek refuge in thee.
2 I say unto Jehovah, "Thou art my Lord,
welfare have I none without thee:
3 As for the saints that are in the land,
and thy noble ones, in them is all my delight."

4 They multiply their sufferings who take another (god) in exchange:
their drink-offerings of blood will I not pour out,
nor take their names upon my lips.
5 Jehovah is the portion of mine inheritance and of my cup;
thou wilt be continually my lot.

6 My measuring-lines have fallen in pleasant places;
   yea, I have a delightsome heritage.
7 I will bless Jehovah, who has given me counsel:
   yea, in the night-seasons mine own reins have admonished me.
8 I have set Jehovah before me continually:
   for he is at my right hand—I shall not be moved.

9 Therefore my heart is glad, and my glory exults,
   my flesh also will dwell in safety.
10 For thou wilt not give up my soul to Hades,
   neither wilt thou suffer thy loving one to see the pit;
11 Thou wilt make known to me the path of life;
   in thy presence is fulness of joys,
   all pleasant things are in thy right hand for ever.

XVIIe. HEARKEN unto innocency, Jehovah;
   attend unto my piercing cry;
   give ear unto my prayer from guileless lips.
2 Let my sentence come forth from thy presence;
   let thine eyes behold uprightly.
3 Thou triest my heart, thou visitest it by night,
   thou assayest me, but canst find no evil device;
   my mouth transgresses not.
4 *   *   *   by the word of thy lips
   I have shunned the ways of the robber.
5 My steps have held fast to thy tracks,
   my feet have not trembled.

6 I have called upon thee, for thou wilt answer me, O God;
   incline thine ear unto me, hear my speech.

7 Make passing great thy kindnesses, O saviour of
    those that flee for refuge
  from them that assail, by thy right hand.
8 Watch over me as the apple of the eye,
  cover me with the shadow of thy wings,
9 From the wicked ones who treat me with violence,
  my greedy enemies, who compass me about.

10 Their caul they have shut tight,
  with their mouth they speak haughtily.
11 At each of our steps they have now surrounded us,
  they set their eyes, till they can hurl us to the
    ground.
12 He is like a lion longing to tear in pieces,
  and as it were a young lion lurking in secret places.

13 Up, Jehovah, intercept him, make him bow down,
  deliver my soul from the wicked by thy sword,
14 From men of the world, whose portion is in life,
  and whose belly thou fillest with thy treasure,
  who are full of sons, and leave their abundance to
    their children.
15 As for me, I shall behold thy face in righteousness;
  may I be satisfied, when I awake, with thine
    image!

XVIIIe. I WILL exalt thee, Jehovah my strength!
2   Jehovah is my high crag and my fortress
    and my deliverer,
  my God, my rock, whereon I take refuge,
  my shield, and my horn of salvation, my sure
    retreat.

3 I call upon him who is to be praised, upon Jehovah,
    and so am I saved from mine enemies.

4 The cords of Death had come about me,
    and torrents of perdition had scared me,
5 The cords of Hades had surrounded me,
    the snares of Death had surprised me.
6 In my strait I called upon Jehovah,
    and cried for help unto my God :
  He heard my voice out of his palace,
    and my cry came before him, even into his ears.

7 Then the earth shook and quaked,
    the foundations also of the hills trembled,
    and shook violently, because he was wroth.
8 There went up smoke at his nostrils,
    and fire out of his mouth devoured,
    coals were set aflame therefrom :
9 And he bowed the heavens and came down,
    with a mass of clouds under his feet.

10 And he rode upon a cherub, and did fly,
    and came swooping upon the wings of the wind :
11 He made darkness his covert,
    round about him as his bower,
    yea, dark waters, clouds of the sky :
12 From the brightness before him there issued forth
    hail-stones and coals of fire.

13 And Jehovah thundered in the heavens,
    and the Most High uttered his voice ;
14 And sent out his arrows and scattered them,
    and lightnings in abundance and confounded them ;

15 And the channels of waters were seen,
    and the foundations of the world were laid bare,
    at thy rebuke, Jehovah,
    at the blast of the breath of thy nostrils.

16 He reached out from high heaven and took me,
    he drew me out of many waters;
17 He delivered me from my fierce enemy,
    and from my haters, for they were too mighty for me;
18 They surprised me in the day of my calamity,
    but Jehovah became my stay;
19 And he brought me forth into a broad place,
    he rescued me, because he delighted in me.

20 Jehovah dealt with me according to my innocence,
    according to the purity of my hands he recompensed me,
21 Because I kept the ways of Jehovah,
    and did not wickedly depart from my God;
22 For all his ordinances were before me,
    and I did not put away his statutes from me;
23 I was also without flaw towards him,
    and I kept myself from guiltiness.

24 So Jehovah recompensed me according to my innocence,
    according to the purity of my hands in his eyesight.
25 With the loving thou shewest thyself loving,
    with the flawless man thou shewest thyself flawless;
26 With him that purifies himself thou shewest thyself pure,
    and with the perverse thou shewest thyself froward;

27 For thou savest afflicted people,
  but haughty eyes thou bringest low.

28 For *thou* lightest my lamp,
  Jehovah my God makes my darkness radiant.
29 For by thee I can break through a fence,
  and by my God I can leap over a wall.
30 As for God, his way is flawless,
  the promise of Jehovah is tried in the fire:
  he is a shield unto all that take refuge in him.

31 For who is God save Jehovah?
  or who is a rock save our God?
32 The God who girt me with strength,
  and rendered my way flawless,
33 Who made my feet like hinds' feet,
  and set me upon my high places,
34 Who trained my hands to war,
  so that mine arms could bend a bow of bronze.

35 Yea, thou gavest me the shield of thy salvation;
  thy right hand held me up,
  and thy humility made me great.
36 Thou madest for me a broad place to walk in,
  that mine ancles did not waver.
37 I pursued mine enemies, and overtook them,
  and turned not again till I had consumed them.
38 I dashed them to pieces that they could not rise,
  but fell under my feet.

39 For thou didst gird me with strength for war,
  thou didst bow down mine assailants under me.
40 Thou madest mine enemies turn their backs unto me,
  and them that hated me I extinguished.

41 They cried, but there was none to save;
   unto Jehovah, but he answered them not.
42 I beat them small as the dust before the wind,
   I emptied them out as the mire of the streets.

43 Thou didst win for me escape out of the strifes of the people,
   thou didst set me to be head of the nations;
   people whom I knew not did serve me.
44 At the hearing of the ear they were obsequious unto me,
   aliens came cringing unto me.
45 The alien folk languished,
   and came trembling out of their holds.

46 Jehovah lives, and blessed be my rock,
   and exalted be the God of my salvation;
47 The God that gave me vengeances,
   and subdued peoples under me,
48 That won for me escape from mine enemies,
   yea, that set me on high above mine assailants,
   that delivered me from the violent man.
49 Therefore will I give thanks unto thee, Jehovah, among the nations,
   and make melody unto thy name:
50 Great salvations gives he unto his king,
   and shews loving kindness unto his anointed,
   to David and to his seed for evermore.

XIXe. THE heavens recount the glory of God,
   and the firmament declares his handiwork.

2 Day unto day is a well-spring of speech,
  and night unto night shews forth knowledge;
4 Their voice has gone out through the whole earth,
  and their words unto the end of the world;

* * * * *

  for the sun has he set a pavilion in them;
5 And he is as a bridegroom going forth from his chamber,
  and rejoices as a mighty man to run his course;
6 From one end of the heavens is his going forth,
  and his circuit unto the ends thereof,
  and there is nothing hidden from his heat.

(Fragment of another Psalm.)

7 The law of Jehovah is perfect, refreshing the soul,
  the testimony of Jehovah is faithful, making wise the simple;
8 The behests of Jehovah are right, rejoicing the heart,
  the commandment of Jehovah is pure, enlightening the eyes;
9 The fear of Jehovah is clean, abiding for ever,
  the ordinances of Jehovah are truthful, and righteous altogether.
10 More to be desired are they than gold, yea, than much fine gold,
  sweeter also than honey or the droppings of the comb.

11 Moreover thy servant gets warning by them,
  in the observance of them is great reward.
12 Lapses—who discerns them?
  from unknown faults absolve thou me.

13 Keep back thy servant also from presumptuous sins,
    let them not have dominion over me:
    then shall I be blameless,
    and absolved from great transgression.
14 Accepted be the words of my mouth and the musing of my heart
    before thee, O Jehovah, my rock and my redeemer.

XX[e]. JEHOVAH answer thee in the day of trouble;
    the name of the God of Jacob be thy sure retreat;
2 Send thee help from the sanctuary,
    and uphold thee from out of Zion;
3 Remember all thine offerings,
    and find thy burnt sacrifice fat;
4 Grant thee according to thy heart,
    and fulfil all thy purpose!
5 We would shout for joy at thy salvation,
    and exult at the name of our God;
    Jehovah fulfil all thy petitions!

6 Now am I sure that Jehovah saveth his anointed,
    he will answer him from his holy heaven
    with the mighty saving acts of his right hand.
7 Some (boast) of chariots, and some of horses,
    but we will boast of the name of Jehovah our God.
8 They must stoop and fall,
    whilst we arise and stand upright.
9 O Jehovah, save the king,
    and answer us when we call.

XXI. JEHOVAH! for thy strength the king is glad;
    and for thy salvation how greatly doth he exult!
2 The desire of his heart hast thou given him,
    and the request of his lips hast thou not withheld.

3 For thou meetest him with blessings of good fortune,
    thou settest on his head a crown of fine gold.
4 He asked life of thee—thou gavest it him,
    even length of days for ever and ever

5 His honour is great through thy salvation,
    glory and grandeur thou layest upon him.
6 For thou makest him most blessed for ever,
    thou cheerest him with joy in thy presence.

7 For the king trusts in Jehovah,
    and through the loving-kindness of the Most High
    he shall be unmoved.
8 Thy hand shall reach all thine enemies,
    thy right hand shall reach them that hate thee.

9 Thou shalt make them as a fiery oven when thou appearest,
    Jehovah shall swallow them up in his wrath, and fire shall devour them:
10 Their fruit shalt thou destroy from the earth,
    and their seed from among the children of men.

11 For though they cause evil to impend over thee,
    and plan a wicked device—they will perform nothing;

12 For thou wilt make them turn their backs,
> with thy bowstrings thou wilt aim against their faces.

13 Exalt thyself, Jehovah, in thy strength;
> we will sing and make melody to thy might.

XXIIe. MY God, my God, why hast thou forsaken me,
> and art far off from my help—from the words of my groaning.
2 My God, I cry in the daytime, but thou answerest not,
> by night also, and have no respite.
3 And yet thou art the holy one,
> who inhabitest the praises of Israel.

4 In thee did our fathers trust,
> they trusted, and thou didst deliver them;
5 Unto thee they cried, and made their escape:
> in thee did they trust, and they were not shamed,
6 But I am a worm and no man,
> a reproach of men and despised of people.
7 All that see me make a mock at me,
> they open wide the lips, they shake the head.

8 "He has rolled it upon Jehovah; let him deliver him;
> let him rescue him, since he delights in him."
9 Yea, but thou art he that took me out of the womb,
> thou didst make me to trust upon my mother's breasts.

10 Upon thee was I cast from the birth,
   thou art my God from my mother's womb.
11 Be not far from me, for trouble is near,
   for there is none to help.

12 Many bulls have come about me,
   strong ones of Bashan have encompassed me.
13 They gape upon me with their mouths,
   as a ravening and roaring lion.
14 I am poured out like water,
   and all my bones are out of joint;
   my heart hath become like wax,
   molten in the midst of my bowels.

15 My palate is dried up like a potsherd,
   and my tongue cleaves to my gums,
   and thou layest me in the dust of Death.
16 For dogs have come about me,
   the crew of evil-doers have closed me round;
   they have dug into my hands and my feet.
17 I can count all my bones:
   as for them, they look, and gaze at me.

18 They part my garments among them,
   and cast lots upon my vesture:
19 But thou, Jehovah, be not thou far off;
   O my strength, speed to my help.
20 Deliver my soul from the sword,
   my darling from the power of the dog.
21 Save me from the lion's mouth,—
   yea, from the horns of the wild oxen thou hast
   (already) answered me.

22 I would fain rehearse thy name unto my brethren,
   in the midst of the congregation will I praise thee.

23 Ye that fear Jehovah, praise him ;
    all ye seed of Jacob, glorify him ;
    and stand in awe of him, all ye seed of Israel :
24 For he has not despised nor abhorred the affliction of the afflicted,
    neither has he hid his face from him,
    but when he cried, he hearkened unto him.

25 From thee is my praise in the great congregation,
    my vows will I pay in the presence of them that fear him.
26 The afflicted shall eat and be satisfied ;
    they that inquire after Jehovah shall praise him ;
    let your heart revive for ever !
27 All the ends of the earth shall remember and return unto Jehovah,
    and all the families of the nations shall bow down before him.
28 For the kingdom is Jehovah's,
    and he is ruler among the nations.
29 All the fat ones of the earth—surely unto him shall they bow down,
    all that have gone down into the dust shall bend the knee before him,
30 And as for him that kept not his soul alive,
    his seed shall be reckoned unto Jehovah ;
31 To the next generation they shall rehearse his righteousness,
    to a people that shall be born, that he hath done nobly.

XXIII. JEHOVAH is my shepherd; I shall not want.
2 In pastures of young grass he maketh me lie down:
   by the waters of resting-places doth he gently lead me.
3 He refreshes my soul;
   he leads me in the right tracks
   for his name's sake.
4 Yea, though I walk through the valley of deadly shade,
   I will fear no evil, for thou art with me:
   thy club and thy staff, they comfort me.
5 Thou furnishest a table before me
   in the presence of my foes;
   thou hast anointed my head with oil,
   my cup runs over.
6 Surely good fortune and loving-kindness shall follow me
   all the days of my life,
   and I shall dwell in the house of Jehovah
   for length of days.

XXIV. THE earth is Jehovah's, and the fulness thereof;
   the world, and they that dwell therein,
2 For it was he that founded it upon the seas,
   and established it upon the floods.

3 Who may ascend the mountain of Jehovah,
   and who may rise up in his holy place?

4 He that has clean hands and a pure heart,
    that has not fixed his desire upon knavery,
    nor sworn deccitfully.
5 He shall receive a blessing from Jehovah,
    even righteousness from the God of his salvation.
6 This is the generation of those that inquire after him,
    of those that seek the face of Jacob's God.

(Fragment of another Psalm.)

7 Lift up your heads, O ye gates,
    yea, lift yourselves up, ye ancient doors,
    that the King of glory may come in.
8 "Who, then, is the King of glory"?
    "Jehovah strong and mighty,
    Jehovah mighty in battle."
9 Lift up your heads, O ye gates,
    yea, lift them up, ye ancient doors,
    that the King of glory may come in.
10 "Who, then, is the King of glory"?
    "Jehovah Sabáoth, he is the King of glory

XXV. UNTO thee, O Jehovah, do I lift up my soul.
2 My God, in thee do I trust, let me not be shamed,
    let not mine enemies triumph over me.
3 Yea, let none that wait for thee be shamed :
    let those be shamed who vainly break their faith.
4 Make me to know thy ways, Jehovah ;
    teach me thy paths.
5 Direct me in thy truthfulness, and teach me,
    for thou art the God of my salvation ;
    for thee have I waited all the day long.

6 Remember thy compassions, O Jehovah,
   and thy loving-kindnesses, for they have been from of old.
7 Remember not the sins of my youth, nor my transgressions:
   according to thy loving-kindness remember them for me,
   for thy goodness' sake, Jehovah.

8 Good and upright is Jehovah,
   therefore will he instruct such as miss their aim in the way.
9 The afflicted will he direct in that which is right,
   yea, the afflicted will he teach his way.
10 All the paths of Jehovah are loving-kindness and truth
   unto such as keep his covenant and his testimonies.
11 For thy name's sake, Jehovah, do thou forgive
   mine iniquity, for it is great.
12 Who, then, is the man that feareth Jehovah?
   him will he instruct in the way that he should choose.
13 He himself shall abide in good fortune,
   and his seed shall inherit the land.
14 The secret of Jehovah is for them that fear him,
   and his covenant for their instruction.

15 Mine eyes are continually toward Jehovah,
   for he shall bring my feet out of the net.
16 Turn thou unto me, and have pity upon me,
   for desolate am I and afflicted.
17 Enlarge the straitness of my heart,
   and bring me out of my distresses.

18 Behold mine affliction and my travail,
and pardon all my sins.
19 Behold mine enemies, for they are many,
and they hate me with cruel hatred.
20 Preserve my soul, and deliver me :
let me not be shamed, for I have taken refuge in thee.
21 Let integrity and uprightness guard me,
for I await thee still.

22 Set Israel free, O God, from all his straitenings.

XXVI. RIGHT me, Jehovah, for I walk still in mine integrity
and trust in Jehovah without wavering.
2 Prove me, Jehovah, and try me ;
assay my reins and my heart.
3 For thy loving-kindness is before mine eyes,
and I walk still in thy truthfulness.
4 I have not sat with men of falsehood,
neither have I converse with dissemblers.
5 I hate the congregation of evil-doers,
and will not sit with the ungodly.
6 I wash my hands in innocency,
and would fain compass thine altar, Jehovah ;
7 That I may proclaim with the voice of thanksgiving,
and tell out all thy wonders.

8 Jehovah ! I love the habitation of thy house,
and the place where thy glory dwells.
9 Take not away my soul with sinners,
nor my life with men of blood ;

10 In whose hands are outrages,
   and their right hand is full of bribes.
11 But as for me, I will walk in mine integrity;
   O set me free, and have pity upon me.
12 My foot stands on even ground;
   in the congregations will I bless Jehovah.

XXVII. JEHOVAH is my light and my salvation;
         whom have I to fear?
   Jehovah is the fortress of my life,
   at whom have I to tremble?
2 When evil-doers came near against me
   to eat my flesh,
   those my foemen and mine enemies
   stumbled and fell.
3 Though a host should encamp against me,
   my heart would not fear;
   though war should rise against me,
   still would I be tranquil.

4 One thing have I asked of Jehovah—
   that is my desire;
   that I may dwell in the house of Jehovah
   all the days of my life,
   to gaze upon the pleasantness of Jehovah,
   and to contemplate his palace.
5 For he treasures me in his bower
   in the day of trouble;
   he covers me in the covert of his tent,
   upon a rock does he exalt me.

6 And now shall my head be exalted above mine enemies
round about me:
fain would I offer in his pavilion
sacrifices of glad shouting,
I would sing and make melody unto Jehovah.

(Probably another Psalm.)

7 Hear, Jehovah, when I cry with my voice,
have pity upon me and answer me.
8 [Hast thou not said unto thy servant,]
"Seek ye my face"?
unto thee my heart hath said,
"Thy face, Jehovah, will I seek."
9 Do not hide thy face from me,
thrust not thy servant aside in anger:
thou hast been my help,
abandon me not, neither forsake me,
O God of my salvation.
10 For my father and my mother have forsaken me,
but Jehovah will take me up.

11 Shew me thy way, Jehovah,
and lead me on an even path
because of mine adversaries.
12 Give me not over unto the greed of my foes:
for false witnesses have risen up against me,
and such as breathe out violence.
13 I am confident of beholding
the goodness of Jehovah in the land of the living.
14 Wait for Jehovah:
be courageous, and let thine heart gather strength,
wait, I say, for Jehovah.

XXVIII. UNTO thee, Jehovah, do I cry,
    my rock, be not deaf unto me,
lest if thou hold thy peace towards me,
    I become like those that have gone down into the pit.
2 Hear the voice of my supplications
    when I cry unto thee for help,
    when I lift up my hands to thy holy chancel.
3 O drag me not away with the ungodly
    and with those that work naughtiness,
    who speak peace to their neighbours,
    while evil is in their hearts.

4 Give them according to their deeds,
    and according to the evil of their practices;
    give them after the work of their hands,
    render to them their deserts.
5 For they give no heed unto the deeds of Jehovah,
    nor unto the work of his hands—
    he shall throw them down, and not build them up.

6 Blessed be Jehovah!
    for he has heard the voice of my supplications.
7 Jehovah is my stronghold and my shield,
    my heart trusted in him, and I was helped;
    therefore my heart dances for joy,
    and with my song will I thank him.
8 Jehovah is a stronghold for his people, and an asylum;
    he is a full salvation for his anointed.
9 Save thy people, and bless thine inheritance;
    feed them, and carry them for evermore.

XXIXᵉ. Ascribe unto Jehovah, O ye sons of God,
　　ascribe unto Jehovah glory and strength.
2 Ascribe unto Jehovah the glory of his name,
　　worship Jehovah in hallowed pomp.

3 The voice of Jehovah is over the waters,
　　the God of glory thunders,
　　Jehovah is over the great waters.
4 The voice of Jehovah is with power;
　　the voice of Jehovah is with majesty.
5 The voice of Jehovah breaks the cedars;
　　yea, Jehovah breaks in pieces the cedars of Lebanon;
6 And Lebanon he makes to skip like a calf,
　　and Sirion like a young wild ox.
7 The voice of Jehovah hews [the oak-trees],
　　[hews them with] flames of fire;
8 The voice of Jehovah shakes the wilderness,
　　Jehovah shakes the wilderness of Kadesh.
9 The voice of Jehovah makes hinds to cast their young,
　　yea, it strips the forests,
　　　　*　　*　　*　　*
　　and in his palace every one saith, Glory.

10 Jehovah has seated himself above the flood,
　　yea, Jehovah sits as King for ever.
11 Jehovah will give strength unto his people,
　　Jehovah will bless his people with peace.

XXX. 1 I WILL extol thee, Jehovah, for thou hast drawn me up.
and not made mine enemies to rejoice over me.
2 Jehovah my God!
I cried unto thee for help, and thou healedst me.
3 Jehovah! thou broughtest up my soul from Hades,
thou recalledst me to life from those that were gone down to the pit.
4 Sing unto Jehovah, O ye his loving ones,
and give thanks to his holy memorial.
5 For a moment passes in his anger,
a life in his favour;
weeping may come to lodge at eventide
but (hark!) a glad cry in the morning.

6 But I—I said in my security,
I shall never be moved.
7 Jehovah, in thy favour
thou hadst set me on strong mountains:
thou didst hide thy face,
and I was confounded.
8 Unto thee, Jehovah, did I cry,
and unto Jehovah I made supplication.
9 "What profit is there in my blood,
in my going down to the pit?
can the dust give thee thanks?
can it declare thy truthfulness?
10 Hear, Jehovah, and have pity upon me:
Jehovah, be a helper unto me."

11 Thou didst turn for me my mourning into dancing,
   thou didst loose my sackcloth, and gird me with joy,
12 To the end that my glory might make melody unto thee without ceasing:
   Jehovah my God, I will give thanks unto thee for ever.

XXXIe. IN thee, Jehovah, have I sought refuge,
   let me never be put to shame:
in thy righteousness rescue thou me.
2 Incline thine ear unto me, deliver me speedily,
   be to me an asylum-rock, a fortified house,
   that thou mayest save me.
3 For thou art my high crag, and my fortress,
   and for thy name's sake thou wilt guide and gently lead me.
4 Bring me out of the net that they have hidden for me,
   for thou art my stronghold.
5 Into thy hand I commend my spirit;
   thou settest me free, Jehovah, thou God of truth.
6 Thou hatest those that give heed to lying vanities,
   but as for me, in Jehovah do I trust.
7 Let me exult and be joyful in thy loving-kindness,
   who sawest mine affliction,
   and tookest notice of the troubles of my soul,
8 And didst not enthrall me under the hand of the enemy,
   but didst plant my feet in a broad place.

9 Have pity upon me, Jehovah, for I am in trouble;
   mine eye is fallen in for vexation,
   my soul and my body [are confounded].

10 For my life is consumed with heaviness,
    and my years with sighing;
    my strength breaks down because of my guilt,
    and my bones are fallen away.
11 Because of all my foes I am become a reproach,
    and to my neighbours a shaking of the head,
    and a terror unto my familiar friends;
    they that saw me without fled away from me.
12 I am cut off, like a dead man, from remembrance,
    I am become like a vessel left to perish.
13 For I have heard the whispering of many,
    a dread is on every side;
    when they conspire together against me
    they devise how to take away my life.

14 And I—on thee, Jehovah, have I trusted;
    I have said, Thou art my God.
15 My times are in thy hand;
    rid me out of the hand of mine enemies and from
        my pursuers.
16 Make thy face to shine upon thy servant;
    save me for thy loving-kindness.
17 Let me not be shamed, O Jehovah, for I have called
        upon thee;
    let the ungodly be shamed, and put to silence in
        Hades.
18 Let the lying lips become mute,
    which speak arrogantly against the righteous
    in haughtiness and scorn.

19 How plenteous is thy goodness, which thou hast
    treasured up for those that fear thee,

which thou hast practised unto them that take refuge in thee
before the sons of men!

20 Thou coverest them in the covert of thy face
from slanderers among men:
thou treasurest them in a bower against the accusing of tongues.

21 Blessed be Jehovah!
for he hath made passing great his loving-kindness unto me in an intrenched city.

22 And I—I had said in mine alarm,
I am cut away from before thine eyes:
but surely thou heardest the voice of my supplications
when I cried for help unto thee.

23 O love Jehovah, all ye his devout ones:
Jehovah keeps faithfulness,
and abundantly recompenses him that deals haughtily.

24 Be courageous, and let your heart gather strength,
all ye that wait for Jehovah.

XXXIIe. HAPPY he whose transgression is forgiven, whose sin is covered.

2 Happy the man to whom Jehovah reckons not iniquity,
and in whose spirit there is no guile.

3 When I kept silence, my bones wasted away
through my roaring all the day long:

4 For day and night thy hand was heavy upon me,
   my tongue was turned as in the droughts of summer.

5 My sin I made known unto thee,
   and mine iniquity I covered not;
  I said, I will confess my transgressions unto Jehovah,
   and thou—thou tookest away the guilt of my sin.

6 Therefore let every devout man pray unto thee in the time of distress:
   at the sound of the overflow of great waters,
   unto such a one they shall not reach.

7 Thou art a covert for me; thou wilt guard me from trouble:
   * * wilt thou surround me.

8 I will instruct thee, and teach thee in the way thou art to go;
   I will give thee counsel, mine eye shall be upon thee.

9 Be ye not like unto horse and mule, without understanding,
   whose mouth must be held with bit and bridle,
   else they approach thee not.

10 Many pains hath the ungodly,
   but he that trusts in Jehovah—
   with loving-kindness will he surround him.

11 Be joyful in Jehovah, and exult, ye righteous;
   and ring out your gladness, all ye upright in heart.

XXXIII. RING out, ye righteous, your gladness in Jehovah;
for the upright praise is seemly.

Give thanks unto Jehovah with the lyre;
with a ten-stringed harp make melody unto him.
3 Sing unto him a new song;
play cunningly with a glad shouting.
4 For the word of Jehovah is straight,
and all his doing is in faithfulness.
5 He loves righteousness and justice:
the earth is full of the loving-kindness of Jehovah.
6 By the word of Jehovah were the heavens made,
and all their host by the breath of his mouth.
7 He gathers the waters of the sea as a harvest-heap,
he lays up the floods in storehouses.
8 Let all the earth fear Jehovah;
of him let all the world's inhabitants be in awe.
9 For *he* spake, and it came into being;
he commanded, and there it stood.
10 Jehovah has brought the purpose of the nations to nought,
he has made the designs of the peoples of none effect.
11 The purpose of Jehovah shall stand for ever,
the designs of his heart unto all generations.
12 Happy the nation whose God is Jehovah,
the people he has chosen for a heritage unto him.
13 Out of heaven looks down Jehovah,
he beholds all the sons of men:
14 From the place of his habitation he gazes
on all the inhabitants of the earth—
15 He who forms all their hearts together,
who gives heed to all their works.
16 The king is not saved by a great force,
a mighty man is not delivered by great strength.
17 The horse is a vain thing to save a man,
neither causeth he any to escape by his great force.

18 Behold, the eye of Jehovah is upon them that fear him,
　　upon them that wait for his loving-kindness;
19 To deliver their soul from death,
　　and to keep them alive in famine.
20 Our soul hopes for Jehovah:
　　he is our help and our shield.
21 For our heart shall rejoice in him,
　　because we have trusted in his holy name.
22 Let thy loving-kindness, Jehovah, brood over us,
　　according as we have waited for thee.

XXXIV. I WILL bless Jehovah at all times:
　　his praise shall be continually in my mouth.
2 My soul shall make her boast in Jehovah,
　　the afflicted shall hear, and rejoice.
3 Magnify Jehovah with me,
　　and let us exalt his name together.
4 I inquired of Jehovah, and he answered me,
　　and delivered me from all my terrors.
5 O look unto him, and ye shall beam with joy,
　　and your face cannot be abashed.
6 This afflicted one cried, and Jehovah heard,
　　and saved him out of all his troubles.
7 The angel of Jehovah encamps round about them that fear him,
　　and sets them at liberty.
8 Taste ye and see that Jehovah is good:
　　happy the man that takes refuge in him.
9 Fear Jehovah, ye his holy ones;
　　For they that fear him want nothing.

10 Young lions pine and suffer hunger,
   but they that inquire after Jehovah cannot want anything good.
11 Come, (my) sons, hearken unto me,
   I will teach you the fear of Jehovah.
12 Who is the man that delights in life,
   that loves many days, to see good fortune?
13 Guard thy tongue from evil,
   and thy lips from speaking guile.
14 Depart from evil, and do good;
   seek peace, and pursue it.
15 The eyes of Jehovah are towards the righteous,
   and his ears are towards their cry.
17 They cry, and Jehovah hearkens,
   and delivers them out of all their troubles.
16 The face of Jehovah is against them that do evil,
   to cut off their memorial from the earth.
18 Jehovah is nigh unto the broken in heart,
   and saves them that are crushed in spirit.
19 Many are the misfortunes of the righteous,
   but Jehovah delivers him out of all:
20 He keeps all his bones,
   not one of them is broken.
21 Misfortune shall slay the ungodly,
   and the haters of the righteous shall be dealt with as guilty.
22 Jehovah sets free the soul of his servants
   and none shall be dealt with as guilty that take refuge in him.

XXXV. Plead my cause, Jehovah, with them that implead me;
fight against them that fight against me.
2 Take hold of shield and buckler,
and stand up as my helper:

3 Draw out also the spear and battle-axe
against them that pursue me;
say unto my soul,
I am thy salvation.

4 Put to shame and dishonour be they that seek my soul;
turned back and abashed be they that devise my hurt:
5 Let them be as chaff before the wind,
and the angel of Jehovah pursuing them.

6 Let their way be dark and slippery,
and the angel of Jehovah thrusting them.
7 For without a cause have they hid for me their net,
without a cause have they digged a pit for my soul.

8 Let ruin come upon him unawares,
and let his net which he hath hidden catch himself:
9 And my soul shall exult in Jehovah:
it shall be full joyous in his salvation.

10 All my bones shall say, Jehovah, who is like unto thee,
who deliverest the afflicted from a stronger than he,
yea, the afflicted and needy from him that spoiled him!

11 Unjust witnesses arise,
   they question me of things that I know not.
12 They reward me evil for good ;
   my soul is bereaved of friends.

13 But I—when they were sick, my clothing was sackcloth,
   I afflicted my soul with fasting,
   and my prayer, mayest thou recompense it into my bosom.
14 I went about as though it had been my friend or my brother,
   I bowed down in mourning weeds, as one that lamented for his mother.

15 But at my fall they rejoice, and gather together :
   strangers whom I know not gather together against me,
   and cry out unceasingly,
16 Among profane mockers   *   *
   they gnash upon me with their teeth.

17 Lord, how long wilt thou look on ?
   recover my soul from their roaring,
   my darling from the young lions.
18 I will give thanks unto thee in the great congregation,
   I will praise thee among much people.

19 Let not them rejoice over me that are for a lie mine enemies,
   they that for no cause hate me—let them not wink with the eye.

20 For it is not peace that they speak;
   but they frame deceitful plots against the quiet in the land;
21 And they open their mouth wide upon me,
   they say, Aha, aha, our eye has seen it.

22 Thou seest, Jehovah, keep not silence,
   Lord, be not far from me.
23 Rouse thee and awake for my just right,
   my God and my Lord, for my cause.

24 Right me, according to thy righteousness, Jehovah my God,
   and let them not rejoice over me.
25 Let them not say in their heart, Aha, so would we have it;
   let them not say, We have swallowed him up.

26 Let them be ashamed and abashed together
   that rejoice at my misfortune:
   let them be clothed with shame and disgrace
   that shew insolence towards me.
27 Let them ring out a glad cry
   that have pleasure in my righteous cause:
   yea, let them say continually, Let Jehovah be magnified,
   who delights in the welfare of his servant;
28 And my tongue shall speak musingly of thy righteousness,
   all the day long of thy praise.

XXXVIe. PLEASANT is transgression to the wicked within his heart;
there is no dread of God before his eyes.
2 For he flatters him, so he imagines,
* * * * *
3 The words of his mouth are mischief and guile,
he has left off to act wisely and well.
4 He devises mischief upon his bed;
he sets himself in no good way;
he does not abhor evil.

5 Jehovah, thy loving-kindness touches the heavens;
thy faithfulness reaches to the clouds.
6 Thy righteousness is like the mountains of God;
thy judgments are (like) the great abyss.
Jehovah, thou savest man and beast:
7 How precious is thy loving-kindness, O God,
that the children of men can take refuge under the shadow of thy wings!
8 They feast upon the fatness of thy house;
and of the river of thy pleasures dost thou give them their drink.
9 For with thee is the fountain of life,
by thy light do we see light.

10 O prolong thy loving-kindness unto them that know thee,
and thy righteousness to the upright in heart.
11 Let not the foot of pride come upon me,
and let not the hand of the wicked make me a wanderer.

12 There are the workers of mischief fallen:
they are thrust down, and are not able to rise.

XXXVIIe. BE not thou incensed at the evildoers,
Neither be thou envious against
them that work injustice;
2 For they shall quickly fade away as the grass,
and wither even as the green herb.

3 Trust thou in Jehovah, and do that which is good,
inhabit the land, and cherish faithfulness;
4 Then shalt thou have sweet pleasure in Jehovah,
and he shall grant thee thy heart's petitions.

5 Roll thy career upon Jehovah,
trust in him, and he shall do nobly,
6 And shall bring forth thine innocence as the light,
and thy just right as the noonday.

7 Be resigned to Jehovah, and wait on for him;
be not incensed at one whose career prospers,
at the man who brings to pass knaveries.

8 Cease from anger, and forsake wrath,
be not incensed—it would lead only to evildoing;
9 For evildoers shall be cut off,
but they that await Jehovah—those shall inherit
the land.

10 Yet a little while, and the ungodly will be gone,
thou shalt look after his place, but he will be
away;

11 But the afflicted shall inherit the land,
   and have sweet pleasure in the abundance of peace.

12 The ungodly plots against the righteous,
   and gnashes upon him with his teeth:
13 The Lord laughs at him,
   for he sees that his day is coming.

14 The ungodly draw the sword and bend their bow
   to slay the afflicted and needy,
   to murder such as are upright in way.
15 Their sword shall enter into their own heart,
   and their bows shall be broken.

16 Better is the righteous man's little
   than the great wealth of many ungodly.
17 For the arms of the ungodly shall be broken,
   but Jehovah upholds the righteous.

18 Jehovah takes notice of the days of the blameless,
   and their inheritance shall be for ever.
19 They shall not be shamed in the evil time,
   and in the days of famine they shall be satisfied.

20 For the ungodly shall perish,
   and Jehovah's enemies shall be as the beauty of
     the pastures:
   they shall vanish as smoke, they shall vanish.

21 The ungodly borrows, and cannot pay it back,
   but the righteous shews pity, and gives.
22 For his blessed ones shall inherit the land,
   but his cursed ones shall be cut off.

23 It comes of Jehovah that a man's steps are established,
 and he takes delight in his way.
24 Though he fall, he shall not be laid prostrate,
 for Jehovah upholds his hand.

25 I have been young, and now am old,
 and I have never seen a righteous man forsaken,
 or his seed begging their bread.
26 He is ever showing pity, and lending,
 and his seed is blessed.

27 Depart from evil, and do good,
 and thou shalt dwell for evermore.
28 For Jehovah is the friend of justice,
 and forsakes not his loving ones.

 The unrighteous shall be destroyed for ever,
  and the seed of the ungodly shall be cut off.
29 The righteous shall inherit the land,
 and dwell therein for ever.

30 The mouth of the righteous speaks musingly of wisdom,
 and his tongue utters just things.
31 The law of his God is in his heart,
 his steps shall not be unsteady.

32 The ungodly watches the righteous,
 and seeks to slay him.
33 Jehovah will not leave him in his hand,
 nor condemn him when he is accused.

34 Wait for Jehovah, and observe his way,
    and he shall exalt thee, that thou inherit the land:
    when the ungodly are cut off, thou shalt see it.

35 I have seen the ungodly as a dread tyrant,
    and spreading himself like a cedar of Lebanon.
36 I passed by, and lo, he was gone:
    yea, I sought him, but he could not be found.

37 Observe the blameless man, and behold the upright,
    how there is a posterity to the man of peace.
38 But transgressors shall be destroyed together:
    the posterity of the ungodly shall be cut off.

39 The salvation of the righteous is of Jehovah:
    he is their stronghold in the time of trouble;
40 And Jehovah helps and delivers them,
    he delivers them from the ungodly, and saves them,
    because they take refuge in him.

XXXVIIIe. JEHOVAH, reprove me not in thine indignation,
    neither correct me in thy hot displeasure.
2 For thine arrows have sunk into me,
    and upon me has sunk thy hand.

3 There is no soundness in my flesh for thy fervent ire,
    no health in my bones because of my sin:
4 For mine iniquities are gone over my head,
    as a heavy burden they are too heavy for me.

5 My weals are become noisome and fester,
   because of my foolishness;
6 I am bent double, I am bowed down greatly,
   I go about in mourning weeds all the day long.

7 For my loins are filled with burning;
   and there is no soundness in my flesh.
8 I am benumbed and crushed exceedingly;
   I roar for the disquiet of my heart.

9 Lord, before thee is all my desire,
   and my sighing is not hid from thee:
10 My heart throbs quickly, my strength has forsaken me,
   even the light of mine eyes is gone from me.

11 My lovers and my friends stand aloof from my plague,
12 And they that seek my soul lay snares;
   and they that are anxious for my harm speak of utter destruction,
   and brood upon deceits all the day long.

13 But I am as a deaf man and hear not,
   and as a dumb man that opens not his mouth.
14 Yea, I am become as a man that hears not,
   and in whose mouth are no rejoinders.

15 Yea, for thee, Jehovah, do I wait,
   Thou wilt answer, O Lord my God.
16 For I said, (I fear) lest they should rejoice over me,
   when my foot wavers they become insolent toward me.

17 For I indeed am ready to fall,
   and my pain is continually before me;

18 (For I have to confess my guilt ;
    I am distressed because of my sin :)

19 Whilst they that without a cause are mine enemies
    are strong,
    and they that hate me lyingly are many in number;
20 They also that render evil for good
    are adverse to me because I follow after good.

21 Forsake me not, Jehovah ;
    O my God, be not far from me.
22 Speed to my help,
    O Lord my salvation.

XXXIX[e]. I SAID, "Let me take heed to my ways,
    that I mistake not with my tongue ;
  let me put a bridle on my mouth
  while the ungodly is still before me."
2 I became mutely resigned, I kept silence afar from
    happiness,
    but my pain was stirred up.
3 My heart was hot within me,
    as I mused, the fire kindled ;
    (at last) I spake with my tongue.
4 "Make me, O Jehovah, to know mine end,
    and the measure of my days, what it is ;
    let me know how short my time is.
5 Behold, thou hast made my days (a few) hand-
    breadths long,
    and my lifetime is as nothing before thee :
    surely all is vanity, every man is a lie.

6 Surely in mere semblance man walks to and fro;
   surely for mere vanity are they so boisterous:
   he heaps up, and cannot tell who shall gather it.
7 And now, Lord, what wait I for?
   my hope is in thee.
8 Deliver me from all my transgressions:
   make me not the reproach of the fool.
9 I am become mute, and open not my mouth,
   for thou hast done it.
10 O remove thy plague from off me;
   I am wasted away with the onset of thy hand.
11 With rebukes for iniquity when thou dost chasten a man,
   thou destroyest, like the moth, his desirable things,
   surely every man is vanity.

12 Hear my prayer, Jehovah, and give ear unto my cry,
   hold not thy peace at my tears:
   for I am a guest with thee,
   and a sojourner like all my fathers.
13 Avert thy frown, that I may gleam again,
   before I go hence, and be no more."

XL. I HAD waited, waited for Jehovah,
      and he inclined (his ear) unto me, and heard my cry.
2 He brought me up also out of the pit of destruction,
   out of the miry swamp,
   and set my feet on a rock,
   made firm my stepping;
3 And he put a new song in my mouth,
   even praise unto our God;

that many should see it, and fear,
and put their trust in Jehovah.

4 Happy the man that hath made Jehovah his trust,
and hath not turned to the proud
and them that are treacherously recreant.
5 In full measure hast thou accomplished, O Jehovah my God,
thy marvels and thy designs concerning us;
there is nothing comparable unto thee:
were I to declare and discourse of them,
they would be too many for numbering.
6 In sacrifice and offering thou hadst no delight,
(but) open ears didst thou make me;
burnt-offering and sin-offering thou didst not require;
7 Then said I, "Lo, I am come;
in the roll of the book it is prescribed unto me;
8 To work out thy pleasure is my delight,
and thy law is deep within me."
9 I have been the herald of righteousness in the great congregation;
lo, I have not restrained my lips,
thou, Jehovah, knowest it.
10 Thy righteousness I have not hid within my heart;
have uttered thy faithfulness and thy salvation;
I have not concealed thy lovingkindness
and thy truth from the great congregation.

11 Thou, too, O Jehovah, restrain not thy compassions from me;
thy lovingkindness and thy truth—
let them guard me continually.

12 For evils past numbering have encompassed me,
>   mine iniquities have overtaken me, so that I cannot see;
>> they are more than the hairs of my head,
>> and my heart hath forsaken me.
13 Be pleased, Jehovah, to deliver me:
> Jehovah, speed to my help.
14 Let them be shamed and abashed together
> that seek my soul to take it away;
> let them be driven back with dishonour
> that delight in my misfortune.
15 Let them be appalled by reason of their shame
> that say unto me, Aha, Aha.
16 Let all those that seek thee rejoice and be glad in thee;
> let such as love thy salvation say continually,
> Jehovah be magnified.
17 And I—the afflicted and needy—
> Jehovah will care for me:
> thou art my help and my deliverer,
> make no tarrying, O my God.

XLI. Happy is he that considers the helpless!
> in the day of misfortune Jehovah will rescue him.
2 Jehovah will preserve him, and keep him alive,
> and he shall be called happy in the land;
>> and do not thou deliver him unto the greed of his enemies.
3 Jehovah will support him upon the bed of languishing:
> as oft as he lies low, thou recoverest him in his sickness.

4 I have said, "O Jehovah, have pity on me:
   heal my soul, for I have sinned against thee."
5 But mine enemies wish me evil,
   "When will he die, and his name perish?"
6 And if one come to see me, he speaks falsehood;
   his heart gathers malice to itself;
   he goes abroad, and speaks.
7 All that hate me whisper together against me,
   against me do they imagine evil,
8 "That which will be his perdition is fixed upon him,
   and now that he lies, he will rise up no more:"
9 Even the man of my peace, in whom I trusted,
   he who did eat of my bread, has become insolent towards me.

10 But thou, Jehovah, have pity on me,
   and raise me up, that I may requite them.
11 By this I am sure thou hast pleasure in me,
   that mine enemy shouts not in triumph over me.
12 And as for me, thou upholdest me in my blamelessness,
   and settest me before thy face for ever.

(Subscription to Book I.)

13 Blessed be Jehovah, the God of Israel,
   From æon to æon!
   Amen and Amen.

BOOK II.

PSALMS XLII. AND XLIIIe.

AS a hind which longs after brooks of water,
  so longs my soul after thee, O God.
2 My soul thirsts for God, for the living God;
  when shall I come and appear before God?
3 My tears have been food to me day and night,
  whilst all day long they say unto me, Where is
    thy God?
4 Let me bethink me of these things, pouring out my
    soul within me,
  how I went along with the throng, and led them
    in procession to the house of God,
  with ringing cries and giving of thanks—a festive
    multitude.
5 Why art thou cast down, O my soul, and why dis-
    quieted within me?
  hope thou in God, for I shall yet thank him
  who is the salvation of my countenance and my
    God.

6 My soul is cast down within me; therefore will I
    call thee to mind
  From the land of Jordan and of Hermon, from the
    hill Mizar.

7 Flood calls unto flood at the sound of thy cataracts:
    all thy breakers and billows have gone over me.
8 (Yet) Jehovah will command his lovingkindness in the daytime,
    and in the night his song shall be with me,
    even a prayer unto the God of my life.
9 Let me say unto God my rock, "Why hast thou forgotten me?
    why go I as a mourner amidst the oppression of the enemy?"
10 As though they broke my bones, my foes reproach me,
    whilst all day long they say unto me, Where is thy God?
11 Why art thou cast down, my soul, and why disquieted within me?
    hope thou in God, for I shall yet thank him
    who is the salvation of my countenance and my God.

IIe. 1 Right me, O God, and plead my cause against a loveless nation;
    from the deceitful and unjust man mayest thou deliver me.
2 For thou art God my stronghold: why hast thou cast me off?
    why go I as a mourner amidst the oppression of the enemy?
3 Send out thy light and thy truthfulness, let them lead me,
    let them bring me unto thy holy hill and to thy dwelling-place.
4 Then will I go in unto the altar of God,
    even unto God my exceeding joy:

and upon the lyre will I give thanks unto thee, O
    God my God.
5 Why art thou cast down, O my soul, and why disquieted within me?
    hope in God, for I shall yet thank him
    who is the salvation of my countenance and my
    God.

XLIV. O GOD, we have heard with our ears,
        our fathers have rehearsed unto us,
    the work thou didst in their days, in the days of
    old.
2 With thy hand thou didst root up nations and plant
    them in,
    didst hew down peoples, and spread *them* abroad.
3 For they conquered not the land by their own sword,
    neither did their own arm save them:
    but thy right hand, and thine arm, and the light
    of thy countenance,
    because thou hadst pleasure in them.

4 Thou thyself art my King, O God;
    command full salvation for Jacob.
5 Through thee can we push down our foes,
    in thy name can we tread down our assailants.
6 For not in my bow do I trust,
    neither can my sword save me,
7 But thou hast saved us from our foes,
    and hast put them to shame that hated us.
8 We make our boast of God all day long,
    and give thanks unto thy name for ever.
9 And yet thou hast cast off and hast disgraced us,
    and goest not forth with our hosts.

10 Thou causest us to turn back from the foe,
   and they that hate us plunder at their will.
11 Thou makest us like sheep for eating,
   and hast scattered us among the nations
12 Thou sellest thy people cheaply,
   and hast not set their prices high.
13 Thou makest us a reproach to our neighbours,
   a mocking and a derision to those around us.
14 Thou makest us a byword among the nations,
   a shaking of the head among the peoples.
15 All the day long is my disgrace before me,
   and the shame of my face hath covered me.
16 At the voice of him that reproaches and reviles,
   at the mien of the enemy and the revengeful.

17 All this is come upon us; yet have we not forgotten thee,
   nor become disloyal to thy covenant;
18 Our heart hath not turned back,
   neither have our steps swerved from thy way,
19 That thou shouldest (therefore) have crushed us down into the place of jackals,
   and covered us with deadly shade.
20 If we had forgotten the name of our God,
   or stretched out our hands to any strange god,
21 Would not God search this out?
   for he knows the secrets of the heart.
22 But nay; for thy sake are we killed all the day long,
   we are accounted as sheep for slaughter.

23 Rouse thee, why sleepest thou, Jehovah?
   awake, cast not off for ever.
24 Wherefore hidest thou thy face,
   forgetting our affliction and oppression?

25 For our soul is bowed down to the dust,
    our body cleaves to the earth.
26 Arise to be our help,
    and set us free for thy lovingkindness' sake.

XLVe. MY heart bubbles with goodly words;
    I address my work unto a king:
be my tongue the pen of a nimble scribe!
2 Beauteous art thou, beauteous, above the sons of men;
    grace is shed over thy lips:
    therefore God has blessed thee for ever.

3 Gird thy sword upon thy thigh, O mighty one,
    even thy glory and thy grandeur.
4 *   *   press on, ride,
    for the sake of good faith, righteousness, and humbleness,
    and thy right hand shall teach thee terrible things.
5 Let thine arrows be sharp
    in the heart of the king's enemies;
    let the peoples fall under thee.

6 As for thy throne, [firm is its foundation,]
    God [has established it] for ever and ever:
    a sceptre of equity is the sceptre of thy kingdom.
7 Thou lovest righteousness and hatest iniquity,
    therefore Jehovah, thy God, has anointed thee
    with the oil of joy above thy fellows.

8 Myrrh and aloes are all thy garments,
    out of the ivory palace stringed instruments make thee glad.

9 Kings' daughters are among thy favourites:
　upon thy right hand stands the consort
　in gold of Ophir.
10 Hearken, O daughter, and behold, and incline thine ear;
　forget also thine own people, and thy father's house;
11 So shall the king long after thy beauty,
　for he is thy Lord, therefore bow down unto him.
12 And unto thee shall they come, O daughter of Tyre, with gifts,
　the richest of people shall sue for thy favour.

13 All glorious is the king's daughter; of pearls
　in ouches of gold is her clothing.
14 In broidered apparel is she led along unto the king:
　a train of virgins her companions is brought unto thee,
15 Led along with all joy and exultation,
　they enter into the king's palace.

16 Instead of thy fathers shall be thy children,
　whom thou mayest make princes in all the earth.
17 I will celebrate thy name throughout all generations,
　therefore shall the peoples give thanks unto thee for ever and ever.

XLVI. GOD is our refuge and stronghold,
　　fully proved as a help in troubles.
2 Therefore will we not fear, though the earth should change,
　and the mountains sink into the heart of the sea.

3 Let the waters thereof roar and foam ;
    let the mountains quake at the insolence thereof.

4 *   *   a river, the arms whereof make glad
    the city of God, the sanctuary of the most High.
5 God is in the midst of her ; she totters not ;
    God shall help her when the morn appears.
6 Nations roar, kingdoms totter :
    he shews his voice ; the earth melts away.
7 Jehovah Sabáoth is with us ;
    our sure retreat is Jacob's God.

8 Come, behold the works of Jehovah,
    who appoints such astonishments in the earth,
9 Who makes wars to cease unto the end of the earth,
    who breaks the bow, and cuts the spear in sunder ;
    who burns the chariot in the fire.
10 "Give up, and be sure that I am God :
    I will exalt myself among the nations,
    I will exalt myself in the earth."
11 Jehovah Sabáoth is with us ;
    our sure retreat is Jacob's God.

XLVIIe. O ALL ye peoples, clap your hands together,
    shout ye unto God in ringing tones.
2 For Jehovah is most high and awful,
    a great king over all the earth.

3 He subdued peoples under us,
    and nations under our feet ;
4 He chose out our inheritance for us,
    the pride of Jacob whom he loved.

5 God is gone up with a shout,
  Jehovah with the sound of the trumpet.
6 Make melody unto God, make melody,
  make melody unto our King, make melody.

7 For God is the King of all the earth;
  (make melody *   *   *;)
8 God is become King over the nations:
  God has seated himself upon his holy throne.

9 Princes of peoples have gathered together
    with the people of Abraham's God:
  for to God belong the shields of the earth,
    greatly is he become exalted.

XLVIII. GREAT is Jehovah, and highly to be praised
  in the city of our God, his holy mountain.
2 Beauteous in elevation, the joy of the whole earth,
  is mount Zion, the city of the great king.
3 God in the palaces thereof
  has made himself known as a sure retreat.

4 For, behold, the kings combined,
    they passed on together.
5 As soon as they saw it, they were amazed,
    they were confounded and scared away.
6 Shuddering took hold of them there,
    pangs, as of a woman in childbirth.
7 By an east wind thou didst break in pieces
    ships of Tarshish.

8 Even as we have heard, so have we seen
   in the city of Jehovah Sabáoth,
   in the city of our God;
   God establisheth it for ever.
9 We thought of thy lovingkindness, O God,
   in the midst of thy temple.
10 According to thy name, O God, so is thy praise
   unto the ends of the earth:
   thy right hand is full of righteousness.

11 Let mount Zion rejoice, let Judah's daughters exult,
   because of thy judgments.
12 Walk about Zion, and make the round of her,
   reckon up the towers thereof.
13 Mark well her rampart,
   study her palaces,
   that ye may tell the next generation,
14 That such a God
   is our God, he it is that shall lead us
   for ever and for ever.

XLIX. HEAR ye this, all ye peoples,
   give ear, all ye dwellers in the world,
2 Both those of low and those of high degree,
   rich and poor alike.
3 My mouth shall speak wisdom,
   and the musing of my heart shall be of understanding.
4 I will incline mine ear to a parable,
   I will open my riddle to the lyre.

5 Wherefore should I fear in the days of misfortune,
   though the malice of my foes surround me,

6 Even of such as trust in their riches,
    and make their boast of their great wealth?
7 Nevertheless none can buy himself off,
    nor give unto God his ransom;
8 (Yea, too costly is the redemption of man's soul,
    and one must let that alone for ever;)
9 So that he should live on perpetually,
    and should not see the pit.
10 Truly, see he must that (even) wise men die,
    the fool and the brutal man alike perish,
    and leave their riches to others.
11 The graves are their houses for ever,
    their dwelling-places for generation after generation;
  [forgotten are] they whose names
    men spoke with honour in the lands.
12 But man in splendour hath no continuance;
    he is become as the beasts that are cut off.

13 This is the fortune of those who have self-confidence,
    and of those who after them applaud their speech.
14 Like sheep, they are folded in Hades;
    death is their shepherd, and their form shall waste away;
  Hades shall be their castle for ever,
    and the upright shall trample upon them in the morning.
15 Nevertheless God shall set free my soul
    from the hand of Hades, when it takes me away.
16 Be not thou afraid, when a man becomes rich,
    when the glory of his house increases;
17 For he will not take away all that, when he dies,
    his glory will not descend after him.

18 Although in his lifetime he bless his soul,
   (and men praise thee that thou doest well unto thyself,)
19 He shall go to the generation of his fathers,
   who shall never see the light.
20 Man, being in splendour but without understanding,
   Is become like the beasts that are cut off.

L. EL Elohim Jehovah has spoken,
       and called the earth from the rising of the sun unto the going down thereof.
2 Out of Zion the perfection of beauty
   God has shone forth.
3 Our God will come, and may not keep silence:
   fire devours before him,
   and around him it is very tempestuous.

4 He calls to the heavens above,
   and to the earth, that he may judge his people.
5 "Gather my loving ones unto me,
   those that have made a covenant with me with sacrifice."
6 And the heavens declare his righteousness,
   for God is about to judge.

7 Hear, O my people, and I will speak,
   O Israel, and I will protest unto thee,
   God, even thy God, am I.
8 Not for thy sacrifices will I reprove thee,
   (truly, thy burnt offerings are continually before me,)

9 I will take no bullock out of thy house,
   nor he-goats out of thy folds.
10 For mine is every beast of the forest,
   the cattle upon the mountains of God.
11 I know all the birds of the mountains,
   and the roamers of the plain are in my mind.
12 If I were hungry, I would not tell thee,
   for mine is the world and the fulness thereof.
13 Would I eat bulls' flesh,
   or drink the blood of goats?
14 Sacrifice unto God thanksgiving,
   and pay thy vows unto the most High;
15 And call upon me in the day of trouble,
   I will rescue thee, and thou shalt glorify me.

16 But unto the ungodly saith God,
   What right hast thou to rehearse my statutes,
   or to take my covenant into thy mouth?
17 Whereas thou hatest correction,
   and castest my words behind thee.
18 If thou sawest a thief, thou hadst pleasure in him,
   and with adulterers was thy portion.
19 Thou hast let thy mouth loose for evil,
   and thy tongue contrives deceit.
20 Thou sittest and speakest against thy brother;
   thou givest a push to thine own mother's son.
21 These things hast thou done, and I kept silence;
   thou imaginedst that I was even like thyself;
   I will reprove thee, and order the facts before thee.

22 O consider this, ye that forget God,
   lest I tear in pieces, and there be none to deliver.
23 Whoso sacrifices thanksgiving, glorifies me,
   and to him that keeps the way will I shew the salvation of God.

LI. **H**AVE pity upon me, O God, according to thy lovingkindness :
according to thy plenteous compassions wipe out mine offences.
2 Wash me throughly from mine iniquity,
and cleanse me from my sin.

3 For I myself acknowledge my transgressions,
and my sin is continually before me.
4 Against thee, thee only, have I sinned,
and done that which is evil in thine eyes,
that thou mightest be justified when thou speakest,
and be clear what time thou judgest.
5 Behold, in iniquity was I brought forth,
and in sin did my mother conceive me.
6 Behold, thou desirest truth in the dark places,
therefore in the secret place make me to know wisdom.
7 Purge me with hyssop, and I shall be clean;
wash me, and I shall be whiter than snow.
8 Make me to hear joy and gladness,
that the bones thou hast crushed may thrill with joy.
9 Hide thy face from my sins,
and wipe out all mine iniquities.

10 Create me a clean heart, O God,
and renew within me a stedfast spirit.
11 Cast me not away from thy presence,
and take not thy holy spirit from me.

12 Restore unto me the joy of thy salvation,
   and uphold me with a willing spirit.
13 Then will I teach transgressors thy ways,
   and sinners shall turn back unto thee.
14 Deliver me from bloodguiltiness, O God, the God of my salvation,
   and my tongue shall ring out thy righteousness.
15 O Lord, open my lips,
   and my mouth shall publish thy praise.
16 For thou hast no pleasure in sacrifices, that I should present them:
   thou favourest not burnt offerings.
17 The sacrifices of God are a broken spirit,
   a broken and a crushed heart, O God, thou canst not despise.

18 Do good in thy favour unto Zion;
   build thou the walls of Jerusalem.
19 Then wilt thou be pleased with the right sacrifices,
   burnt offering and whole burnt offering;
   then will they offer bullocks upon thine altar.

LII. Why gloriest thou in mischief, O mighty man?
   God's lovingkindness perpetually endures.
2 Thy tongue devises destruction,
   like a whetted razor, O thou that workest guile.
3 Thou lovest evil more than good;
   lying rather than to speak righteousness.
4 Thou lovest all devouring words;
   *   *   a deceitful tongue.

5 God in return shall pull thee down for ever,
   shall gripe thee fast, and pluck thee out of thy tent,
   and root thee out of the land of the living.
6 The righteous shall see it, and fear,
   and shall laugh at him:
7 " Lo, there is the man that made not God his stronghold,
   but trusted in his great wealth, and felt strong in his substance."
8 But I am like a fresh-green olive-tree in the house of God;
   I trust in the lovingkindness of God for ever and ever.
9 I will give thanks unto thee for ever, for thou hast done nobly,
   and declare before thy loving ones that thy name is good.

PSALM LIII.
A repetition of Psalm XIV.

LIV. O GOD, save me by thy name,
       and right me by thy strength.
2 O God, hear my prayer,
   give ear to the words of my mouth.
3 For strangers are risen up against me,
   and tyrants seek my soul,
   not setting thee before their eyes.

4 Behold, God is my helper;
   the Lord is among them that uphold my soul.

5 Let their evil return unto my foes :
  do thou extinguish them in thy truthfulness.
6 I will sacrifice unto thee with a free will,
    and give thanks unto thy name, Jehovah, because it is good.
7 For he has delivered me out of all trouble,
  and mine eye has looked its full upon mine enemies.

LVe. GIVE ear to my prayer, O God;
   And hide not thyself from my supplication :
2 Attend unto me and answer me ;
  I have no rest in my complaint, and moan aloud,
3 For the sound of [the revilings of] the enemy,
  because of the cries of the ungodly :
  for they are ever hurling mischief at me,
  and in wrath they persecute me.
4 My heart is sore pained within me,
  and deadly terrors have fallen upon me.
5 Fearfulness and trembling penetrate into me,
  and a horrible dread infolds me.
6 Then I said, "Oh that I had wings like a dove !
  I would fly away and abide :
7 Lo, then would I flit far away,
  and lodge in the wilderness.
8 I would speed unto him that gives me escape
  from the stormy wind and tempest."

9 Swallow up, Jehovah ; divide their speech :
  for I behold violence and strife in the city.
10 Day and night they make their rounds on the walls thereof :
   trouble and mischief are in the midst of it.

11 Very destruction is in the midst thereof:
   oppression and guile depart not from its forum.
12 (For it was not an enemy that reproached me—that I could have borne;
   nor was it my hater that was insolent towards me, then I might have hid myself from him.
13 But it was thou, a man mine equal,
   mine associate and my familiar friend;
14 Together we held sweet fellowship,
   and walked to the house of God in the throng.)

15 Let death steal upon them; let them go down alive into Hades:
   for wickedness is in their dwelling, yea, within them.
16 As for me, I will call upon God;
   and Jehovah shall save me.
17 Evening, and morning, and at noon will I complain and make my moan:
   and he shall hear my voice.
18 He hath set free my soul in peace that they might not come nigh me,
   for in great numbers were they against me.
19 God shall hear [the cry of the afflicted],
   and he that is enthroned of old shall answer them.

(Here follows a misplaced portion of this or of another Psalm.)

* * * * *

20 To whom come no changes,
   and who fear not God.
21 He has laid his hands upon those at peace with him,
   he has desecrated his covenant.

22 His mouth is smoother than butter,
  but his heart is all war;
  his words are softer than oil,
  and yet are they drawn swords.
23 Cast thy burden upon Jehovah,
  and he will support thee;
  he will not always appoint tottering for the righteous.
24 And thou, O God, shalt cast them down into the pit of the grave:
  bloody and deceitful men shall not live out half their days,
  But I—will trust in thee.

LVIe. HAVE pity upon me, O God, for mortal men do crush me;
  fighting daily they oppress me.
2 Mine adversaries do crush me all the day long,
  yea, many are they that with high looks do fight against me.
3 On the day when I might fear I will trust in thee.
4 Through God can I praise his word,
  in God will I trust without fear:
  what can flesh do unto me?

5 All day long they torture my words:
  all their thoughts are against me for evil.
6 They make invasion and set an ambush;
  themselves they mark my footprints,
  according as they have long since waited for my soul.
7 *   *   *   *
  In anger do thou cast the peoples down, O God.

8 My wanderings thou thyself hast reckoned,
    my tears are put into thy bottle,
    surely they are in thy reckoning.
9 Then shall mine enemies turn back,
    in the day that I call;
    this I know, that God is for me.
10 Through God can I praise his word:
11 In God will I trust without fear:
    what can man do unto me?
12 Vows made unto thee are upon me, O God:
    I will render thank-offerings unto thee.
13 For thou hast delivered my soul from death,
    yea, my feet from stumbling,
    that I may walk before God in the light of life.

LVII.

HAVE pity upon me, O God, have pity upon me,
    for in thee my soul has taken refuge,
    yea, in the shadow of thy wings will I take refuge,
    until the destruction be overpast.
2 I will call unto God most high,
    unto the Strong One that deals bountifully with me.
3 He shall send from heaven and save me;
    when he that would crush me reproaches, God shall send forth
    his lovingkindness and his truth.
4 With my soul must I lie down in the midst of lions,
    fire-breathers are the sons of men,
    their teeth are spears and arrows,
    and their tongue a sharp sword.
5 Exalt thyself, O God, above the heavens,
    and thy glory above all the earth.

6 They have prepared a net for my feet;
   they have bowed down my soul—they have digged before me
   a pit into whose midst they have fallen!
7 Stedfast is my heart, O God, stedfast is my heart;
   I would sing and make melody.
8 Awake, my glory; awake, harp and lyre;
   fain would I awaken the dawn.
9 I will give thanks unto thee, O Lord, among the peoples,
   I will make melody unto thee among the nations:
10 For thy lovingkindness is great unto the heavens,
   and thy truth unto the clouds.
11 Exalt thyself, O God, above the heavens,
   and thy glory above all the earth.

LVIII\[e\]. DO ye indeed speak righteousness, O ye gods?
   do ye judge in equity the sons of men?
2 Nay, but ye all prepare wickedness;
   ye weigh out in the land the violence of your hands.
3 The ungodly are estranged from the womb:
   they have gone astray from their birth, speaking lies.
4 They have poison as the poison of a serpent:
   yea, as that of a deaf adder which stops her ear;
5 Which will not hearken to the voice of charmers,
   Nor of the most cunning binder of spells.

6 Break their teeth, O God, in their mouth:
    tear out the jawbones of the young lions, Jehovah.
7 Let them melt as water that runs away;
    as grass, let them be quickly cut off:
8 [Let them be] as a snail melting as it goes along,
    as the untimely born of a woman which never saw the sun.
9 Before your pots can feel the thorns,
    and while your flesh is still raw,
    the hot wrath (of Jehovah) shall sweep it away.

10 The righteous shall rejoice that he has seen vengeance,
    he shall wash his feet in the blood of the ungodly;
11 And men shall say, Truly there is a fruit for the righteous,
    truly there are divine powers that judge in the earth.

LIXe. DELIVER me from mine enemies, O my God,
    set me secure from them that assail me:
2 Deliver me from the workers of naughtiness,
    and save me from the men of blood.
3 For lo they lie in wait for my soul;
    fierce (invaders) attack me
    without any transgression or sin of mine, Jehovah.
4 Without my fault they run and take their place;
    awake thou to meet me, and behold.
5 Thou therefore, Jehovah Sabáoth, Israel's God,
    rouse thee to visit all the nations;
    have no pity on all these wicked traitors.

6 They come evening after evening, they snarl like dogs,
    and make their round in the city.
7 Behold, they belch out with their mouth,
    swords are in their lips,
    for "Who hears"?
8 But thou, Jehovah, laughest at them,
    thou mockest at all the nations.
9 My strength, unto thee will I make melody,
    for God is my sure retreat.

10 My God shall meet me with his lovingkindness,
    God shall let me look my fill upon mine enemies.
11 Slay them not, lest my people forget;
    make them wanderers by thy power,
    and cast them down, O Lord our shield.
12 Their mouth sins by each word of their lips,
    therefore let them be taken in their pride,
    and for the cursing and lying which they talk.
13 Make an end in wrath, make an end, that they be no more,
    and let them know that God' is ruler in Jacob,
    unto the ends of the earth.

14 And they come evening after evening, they snarl like dogs,
    and make their round in the city.
15 They indeed wander about to devour,
    they murmur if they be not satisfied;
16 But I will sing of thy strength,
    and will ring out thy lovingkindness in the morning,
    for thou hast been unto me a sure retreat
    and a refuge in the day of my trouble.

17 My strength, unto thee will I make melody,
    for God is my sure retreat,
    the God of my lovingkindness.

LXe. O GOD, thou hast cast us off and scattered us,
    thou hast been angry, O vouchsafe to restore us!
2 Thou hast made the land to quake; thou hast cleft it,
    heal the breaches thereof, for it totters.
3 Thou hast let thy people see hard things;
    thou hast made us to drink the wine of reeling.
4 Thou hast given a banner to them that fear thee,
    (only) that they may flee before the bow.
5 That thy beloved ones may be delivered,
    save with thy right hand, and answer us.

6 God has promised by his holiness; let me exult;
    I am to divide Shechem, and mete out the valley of Succoth.
7 Mine is Gilead and mine Manasseh,
    Ephraim also is the defence of my head;
    Judah is my staff of command:
8 Moab is my washpot, over Edom will I cast out my shoe:
    over Philistia is my triumph.

9 Who will bring me into the entrenched city?
    who will lead me into Edom?
10 Surely thou, O God, hast cast us off,
    and goest not forth, O God, with our armies.

11 O give us help from trouble,
    for vain is man's deliverance.
12 Through God we shall do valiantly,
    and it is he that shall tread down our foes.

LXI. **HEAR** my cry, O God,
    attend unto my prayer.
2 From the end of the earth do I cry unto thee
    when my heart faints,
    lead me on to the rock that is too high for me.
3 For thou hast been a refuge to me,
    a strong tower against the enemy.
4 Let me sojourn in thy pavilion for ever,
    let me take refuge in the hiding-place of thy wings.

5 For thou, O God, hast hearkened to my vows,
    thou hast granted the heritage of those that fear thy name.
6 Mayest thou prolong the king's life,
    may his years be for generations on generations.
7 May he sit before God for ever,
    appoint (thy) lovingkindness and truthfulness to guard him.
8 So will I make melody unto thy name for ever,
    that I may perform my vows day by day.

LXIIe. **MY** soul, be simply resigned to God;
    from him comes my salvation.
2 He alone is my rock and my salvation,
    my sure retreat—I shall not be shaken.

3 How long will ye be frantic against (one) man,
    will ye be dashing in pieces all of you—
    as it were a toppling wall, a fence pushed-in.
4 They only consult how to thrust him from his dignity,
    they delight in lies, they each of them bless with
        the mouth,
    but inwardly they curse.

5 My soul, be simply resigned to God,
    for from him comes my expectation.
6 He alone is my rock and my salvation,
    my sure retreat—I shall not be shaken.

7 Upon God rests my salvation and my honour;
    the rock of my stronghold and my refuge are—
        God.
8 Trust in him at all times, ye people;
    pour out your heart before him;
    God is a refuge for us.

9 Simply a breath are men of low degree, the lordly
        are simply a lie;
    being weighed in the balances, they are altogether
        as a breath.
10 Trust not in perverseness, neither become as a breath
        by crookedness:
    if riches increase, take no heed thereto.
11 God hath spoken once; twice have I heard this;
    that strength belongs unto God:
12 Thine, too, Jehovah, is lovingkindness,
    for thou renderest unto every man according to
        his work.

LXIIIe. O GOD, thou art my God; earnestly do I
seek thee;
my soul thirsts for thee, my flesh pines for thee
in a dry and fainting land where no water is;
2 In such wise do I long for thee, in the sanctuary
to behold thy power and glory.

3 For thy lovingkindness is better than life itself;
my lips shall praise thee.
4 In such wise will I bless thee while I live,
and lift up my hands in thy name.

5 My soul shall be satisfied as with marrow and fatness,
and with mirthful lips shall my mouth sing praise.
6 When I call thee to mind upon my bed,
in the night watches do I meditate upon thee.

7 For thou hast been my help,
and in the shadow of thy wings do I shout for joy.
8 My soul clings fast after thee:
thy right hand upholds me.

9 As for them, they seek my soul to destroy it:
they shall enter into the nether world.
10 They shall be given up into the grasp of the sword;
they shall be the portion of jackals.
11 But the king shall rejoice in God;
every one that swears by him shall glory:
for the mouth of them that speak lies shall be
stopped.

LXIV. HEAR my voice, O God, in my complaint:
guard my life from fear of the enemy.
2 Hide me from the conspiracy of the wicked,
from the throng of them that work naughtiness;
3 Who have whet their tongue like a sword,
and stretched their arrow—a bitter speech,
4 That they may shoot in their hiding-places at the blameless,
suddenly shoot at him, and not be afraid.

5 They put all their strength into an evil matter;
they discourse of hiding snares,
they ask who looks at them.
6 They think out knaveries, [and say,]
"we have accomplished a well thought out thing,"
and the inward part of each one [is unsearchable],
and the heart [of every one] is deep.

7 But *God* shall shoot at *them* with an arrow;
suddenly shall they be wounded.
8 *   *   *   *   *
all that look upon them shall shake the head;
9 And all men shall fear and shall declare God's work,
and shall understand his operation.
10 The righteous shall rejoice in Jehovah, and take refuge in him,
and all the upright in heart shall glory.

LXV. MEET for thee, O God, is praise in Zion,
and unto thee let the vow be performed.
2 O thou that hearest prayer,
unto thee let all flesh come.
3 Guilty deeds are too mighty for me:
our transgressions—vouchsafe to cancel them!
4 Happy is he whom thou choosest and causest to approach,
that he may abide in thy courts:
fain would we have our fill of the goodness of thy house,
even of thy holy temple.

5 With terrible things in righteousness dost thou answer us,
O God of our salvation;
thou confidence of all the ends of the earth,
and of the nations afar off:
6 Who establishes the mountains by his force,
being girded with might:
7 Who stills the roaring of the seas,
the roaring of their billows, and the tumult of the peoples;
8 So that upon those who dwell at the ends comes fear at thy signs,
the sources of morning and evening thou fillest with ringing cries.
9 Thou hast visited the earth and makest her overflow:
thou greatly enrichest her;

the river of God is full of water;
thou preparest their corn, for thus fully thou preparest her.
10 Thou waterest her furrows, thou smoothest down her ridges,
thou softenest her with showers, thou blessest all that springs of her.

11 Thou hast crowned the year of thy goodness,
and thy tracks drop fatness.
12 The pastures of the wilderness drop,
and the hills are girt with dancing joy.
13 The meadows are clothed with flocks,
and the valleys are covered with corn;
they shout for joy; yea, they sing.

LXVIe. SHOUT ye merrily unto God, all ye upon earth,
2 Make melody unto the glory of his name,
ascribe glory to praise him.
3 Say unto God, How terrible are thy works!
so great is thy strength that thine enemies cringe unto thee.
4 All upon the earth shall worship thee,
and make melody unto thee, make melody unto thy name.
5 Come ye and see the works of God,
how terrible he is in his doing towards the sons of men.
6 He turned the sea into dry land;
they went on foot through the river—
there let us rejoice in him.

7 He rules by his might for ever;
   his eyes survey the nations:
   let not the rebellious deal so proudly.

8 O bless our God, ye peoples,
   and make the sound of his praise to be heard,
9 Who has set our soul in life,
   and has not suffered our foot to waver.
10 For thou, O God, hast proved us:
   thou hast refined us, as silver is refined.
11 Thou broughtest us into the hold;
   thou laidest a crushing weight upon our loins.
12 Thou didst cause mortal men to ride over our heads;
   we went through fire and through water,
   but thou broughtest us out into a place of liberty.

13 I will go into thy house with burnt offerings,
   I will render unto thee my vows,
14 Such as escaped from my lips,
   and my mouth did utter, when I was in straits.
15 Burnt offerings of fatlings will I offer unto thee,
   with the sweet smoke of rams;
   I will sacrifice bullocks with goats.

16 Come ye, hearken, and let me rehearse, all ye that
    fear God,
   that which he did for myself.
17 I cried unto him with my mouth,
   and a lofty hymn was (already) under my tongue.
18 If I have intended iniquity in my heart,
   the Lord will not hear me;
19 But verily God has heard,
   he has been attentive to the sound of my prayer.
20 Blessed be God, who has not withdrawn
   my prayer and his lovingkindness from me.

LXVII. MAY God be gracious unto us and bless us,
    may he cause his face to shine upon us,
2 that thy way may be known upon earth,
    even thy salvation among all nations.

3 Let the peoples give thanks unto thee, O God;
    let the peoples all of them give thanks unto thee.
4 Let the nations rejoice with ringing cries,
    for thou wilt judge the peoples in equity,
    and lead the nations upon earth.
5 Let the peoples give thanks unto thee, O God,
    let the peoples all of them give thanks unto thee.

6 The earth has yielded her increase;
    may God, our own God, bless us.
7 May God bless us;
    and let all the ends of the earth fear him.

LXVIIIe. LET God arise, let his enemies be scattered,
    and let them that hate him flee before him.
2 As smoke is driven away, so mayest thou drive them away:
    as wax melts before the fire,
    so let the ungodly perish at the presence of God.
3 But let the righteous rejoice and triumph
    before Jehovah, and be merry and joyful.

4 Sing unto God, make melody unto his name,
   cast up a way for him who rides through the deserts,
   whose name is Jah, and triumph before him—
5 Who is a father of the orphans, and an advocate of
      the widows,
   even God in his holy habitation.
6 God gives the desolate a home :
   he brings out the prisoners into prosperity,
   the rebellious notwithstanding dwell in a parched
      land.

7 O God, when thou wentest forth before thy people,
   when thou marchedst through the wilderness,
8 The earth quaked, the heavens also dropped,
   at the presence of God yonder Sinai [shook],
   at the presence of God, the God of Israel.
9 A liberal rain didst thou shed, O God,
   upon thine inheritance [so fainting] and weary,
   thou didst raise up [the dry land].
10 Thy living creatures settled therein :
   thou preparedst for the poor in thy goodness, O
      God.

11 The Lord gave the word :
   the heraldesses of victory were a great host.
12 "Kings of hosts flee—they flee,
   and she that has tarried at home divides the
      spoil."
13 *   *   *   *
               *   *   *
               *   *   *
14 When Shaddai scattered kings therein,
               *   *   *

15 God's mountain-range is the range of Bashan,
   a mountain-range with peaks is the range of Bashan.
16 Why look ye askance, ye mountains with peaks,
   on the mount which God has desired to dwell in?
   yea, Jehovah will abide there for ever.
17 The chariots of God are myriads twice-told, * *
   *   *   *   *   *
18 Thou hast gone up into the height to abide;
   O Jah, thou hast carried away captives, thou hast received
   gifts of men, yea, and also of the rebellious.

19 Blessed be the Lord!
   day by day he bears our burdens—
   the God of our salvation.
20 God is unto us a God of salvations,
   and unto Jehovah belong escapes from death.
21 Notwithstanding God will shatter the head of his enemies,
   the hairy scalp of him who goes on in his guiltinesses.
22 The Lord said, I will bring (them) back from Bashan,
   I will bring (them) back from the ocean-gulfs,
23 That thou mayest wash thy foot in blood,
   that the tongue of thy dogs may have its portion from the enemies.

24 They have seen thy progress, O God,
   the progress of my God, my King, into the sanctuary.
25 Singers went before, minstrels followed after,
   In the midst of damsels playing on timbrels.

26 In the congregations bless ye God,
    even the Lord, ye who are of the fountain of Israel.
27 There is Benjamin the little   *   *
    the princes of Judah   *   *
    the princes of Zebulun, the princes of Naphtali.

28 Command thy strength, O God;
    strengthen, O God, that which thou hast wrought for us.
29 *   *   *   *   *
    from thy temple unto Jerusalem;
    kings shall bring presents unto thee.
30 Rebuke the beasts of the reeds, the troop of bulls,
    tread under thee the calves of the peoples, those that delight in silver,
    scatter the peoples that have pleasure in wars.
31 Princes shall come out of Egypt;
    Ethiopia shall quickly stretch out her hands to God.

(Israel's preaching to the kingdoms.)

32 Ye kingdoms of the earth, sing unto God,
    make melody unto the Lord.
33 [Extol] him that rides through the ancient heaven of heaven;
    behold, he utters his voice, and that a mighty voice.
34 Ascribe ye strength unto God over Israel;
    whose majesty and strength are in the clouds.

(The reply of the kingdoms.)

35 Awful is God's ruling from out of thy sanctuary;
    the God of Israel—it is he that gives strength and mightiness to his people; blessed be Jehovah.

LXIXe. SAVE me, O God;
for the waters are come in even to the soul.
2 I am sunk in the mire of a gulf
where there is no standing;
I am come into watery depths,
where the stream overwhelms me.
3 I am wearied with my crying, my throat is burnt up,
mine eyes fail while I wait for my God.
4 They that hate me without a cause are more than the hairs of my head,
they that are lyingly mine enemies are more in number than my bones;

* * * *

that which I had not robbed, I had to restore.
5 O God, thou knowest my foolishness,
and my guiltinesses are not hid from thee.
6 Let not them that wait for thee be shamed in me;
let not those that seek thee be dishonoured in me,
O God of Israel.

7 For it was for thee that I bore reproach,
dishonour covered my face;
8 I became a stranger unto my brethren,
and an alien unto my mother's children:
9 Because zeal for thy house consumed me,
and the reproaches of them that reproached thee fell upon me.
10 I humbled my soul with fasting,
and it served for my reproach.

11 I made sackcloth also my vesture,
    and became a proverb unto them;
12 They that sit in the gate take me for their theme,
    and of me are the carols of the revellers.

13 But as for me, my prayer is unto thee, O Jehovah,
    in a favourable time, O God, because of thine abundant kindness;
    answer me in the stedfastness of thy salvation.
14 Deliver me out of the mire, that I sink not,
    let me be delivered from them that hate me, and out of the watery depths.
15 Let not the rushing stream overwhelm me,
    neither let the gulf swallow me up,
    and let not the pit shut her mouth upon me.
16 Answer me, Jehovah, for thy lovingkindness is good;
    according to thy plenteous compassions turn towards me.
17 And hide not thy face from thy servant;
    for I am in straits: answer me speedily.
18 Draw nigh unto my soul and release it:
    O set me free, because of mine enemies.
19 *Thou* knowest my reproach and shame and dishonour:
    before thee are all my foes.
20 Reproach has broken my heart, and it is very sick;
    I looked for sympathy, but there was none,
    and for comforters, but I found none.
21 For they gave me gall as my food,
    and in my thirst they would have me drink vinegar.

22 Let their table before them become a snare,
    and to the tranquil let it become a trap.

23 Let their eyes be darkened, that they see not;
 and make their loins continually to shake.
24 Pour out thy fervent ire upon them,
 and let thy hot anger overtake them.
25 Let their encampment be desolate,
 let there be none to dwell in their tents.
26 For they persecute him whom *thou* hast smitten,
 and they add to the pain of those whom thou hast wounded.
27 Put on iniquity to their iniquity,
 and let them not come into thy righteousness.
28 Let them be wiped out of the book of life,
 and not be written with the righteous.
29 And as for me, I am afflicted and sore pained;
 let thy salvation, O God, set me secure.

30 I will praise the name of God with a song,
 and magnify him with thanksgiving;
31 And it shall please Jehovah better than an ox,
 better than a bullock with horns and hoofs.
32 The afflicted, seeing it, shall rejoice;
 ye that inquire after God, let your heart revive:
32 For Jehovah hearkens to the needy,
 and despises not his prisoners.
33 Let heaven and earth praise him,
 the seas, and all that moves therein.
34 For God will save Zion,
 and build the cities of Judah;
 and men shall dwell there and have it in possession.
35 The seed also of his servants shall inherit it,
 and they that love his name shall abide therein.

PSALM LXX.
(A repetition of Psalm XL., 13-17.)

LXXIe. MY God, deliver me from the hand of the ungodly,
from the grasp of the unjust and violent man.
5 For thou art my hope, O Lord Jehovah,
my confidence from my youth.
6 On thee have I been stayed from the birth;
thou art he that loosed me from my mother's womb;
of thee is my praise continually.

7 I am become as a prodigy unto many;
but thou art my strong refuge
8 Let my mouth be filled with thy praise,
even with thy glory all the day long.
9 Cast me not away in the time of old age;
forsake me not when my strength fails me.

10 For mine enemies speak concerning me,
and they that watch my soul take counsel together,
11 Saying, "God has forsaken him, set on,
and seize him, for there is none to deliver."
12 O God, be not far from me,
my God, speed to my help.

13 Put to shame and dishonour be the adversaries of my soul,
let them be covered with reproach and dishonour that seek my hurt.

14 But as for me, I will wait on continually,
    and will add to all thy praise.
15 My mouth shall rehearse thy righteousness,
    yea, thy salvation all the day long,
    for I know not the numbers thereof.
16 I will exhibit the mighty acts of the Lord Jehovah;
    I will celebrate thy righteousness, even thine only.

17 O God, thou hast taught me from my youth up,
    and hitherto have I made known thy wondrous works:
18 And even unto old age and grey hairs,
    O God, forsake me not;
    until I have made known thine arm to the next generation,
    thy might unto all that are to come.

19 *   *   *
    and thy righteousness, O God, unto high heaven;
    O thou who hast done great things,
    God, who is like unto thee?
20 Thou, who hast let us see troubles great and sore,
    wilt revive us again,
    and bring us up again from the abysses of the earth.

21 O multiply my greatness, and turn to comfort me.
22 I also will give thanks unto thee with the harp,
    even unto thy truthfulness, O my God;
    I will make melody unto thee with the lyre,
    O thou Holy One of Israel.
23 My lips shall ring out their joy, when I make melody unto thee,
    and my soul which thou hast redeemed.

24 My tongue also shall speak musingly of thy righteousness all the day long,
    because they are ashamed, because they are abashed, that sought my hurt.

LXXIIe. GIVE the king thy judgments, O God,
    and thy righteousness unto the king's son.
2 May he give doom to thy people in righteousness,
    and to thine afflicted ones according to right.
3 May the mountains bear the fruit of peace to the people,
    and the hills through righteousness.
4 May he judge the afflicted of the people,
    save the children of the needy,
    and crush the oppressor.

5 Let them fear him as long as shines the sun,
    and the moon, generation after generation.
6 May he come down like rain upon the meadow;
    like showers may he water the earth.
7 In his days may the righteous flourish,
    and abundance of peace, until the moon be no more.
8 Let him have dominion also from sea to sea,
    and from the river unto the ends of the earth.

9 Before him let foemen bow,
    and let his enemies lick the dust.
10 Let the kings of Tarshish and the far countries bring presents,
    let the kings of Sheba and Seba offer gifts.

11 Let all kings fall down before him,
  let all nations do him service.

12 Because he delivers the needy when he cries,
  the afflicted also who has no helper;
13 He feels for the helpless and needy,
  and the souls of the needy he saves;
14 From injury and violence he releases their soul,
  and costly is their blood in his sight.
15 May he live on, and there be given him of the gold
    of Sheba;
  and let prayer be made for him continually,
  all day long let them bless him.

16 May abundance of corn be in the land,
   upon the top of the mountains may it wave;
   [and the people]—like Lebanon be its fruit,
   and may they blossom out of the city like the
     herb of the earth.
17 Be his name [blessed] for ever;
   while shines the sun, may his name have offspring;
   may all tribes of the earth bless themselves by
     him,
   may all nations call him happy.

(Subscription to Book II.)

18 Blessed be Jehovah, God, the God of Israel,
  who alone does wondrous things;
19 And blessed be his glorious name for ever,
  and let the whole earth be filled with his glory!
                            Amen and Amen.

BOOK III.

PSALM LXXIII.

TRULY God is gracious unto Israel,
  Even unto the pure in heart;
2 But as for me, my feet had almost swerved,
  my steps had almost slipped.

3 For I was incensed at the boasters,
  when I saw the welfare of the ungodly:
4 For nothing have they to torment them;
  sound and stalwart is their strength.

5 They partake not of the travail of mortals,
  neither are they plagued like other men:
6 Therefore pride is about them as a necklace;
  violence covers them as a garment.

7 Out of the caul their iniquity cometh forth;
  the imaginations of their heart overflow:
8 They mock, and speak wickedly of oppression;
  they speak from on high.

9 They have set their mouth in the heavens,
  and their tongue goes about in the earth.

10 Therefore his people are satisfied with bread,
    and water in full measure is supped up by them;

11 And they say, "How should God know?
    and is there knowledge in the most High?
12 Behold, the men yonder are ungodly,
    and secure for ever, they have won great substance.

13 Verily in vain have I cleansed my heart,
    and washed my hands in innocency.
14 And yet I was plagued all the day,
    and my chastisement came every morning."

15 If I had said, "Let such be my discourse,"
    I should have been a traitor to the generation of thy children.
16 But when I considered this, to comprehend it,
    it was travail in mine eyes;

17 Until I went into the sanctuary of God,
    and gave heed unto their future.
18 Surely thou dost set them in slippery places,
    thou castest them down into ruins.

19 How are they brought to desolation in a moment,
    utterly swept off by calamities!
20 As a dream when one has awaked,
    so, Lord, when thou art aroused, thou wilt despise their semblance.

21 Truly my heart had become soured,
    and I had pierced myself to my reins.
22 I indeed was brutish and ignorant,
    I was (like) the beasts towards thee.

23 And yet I am continually with thee;
   thou hast taken hold of my right hand.
24 According to thy purpose wilt thou lead me,
   and afterward receive me with honour.

25 Whom have I (to care for) in heaven?
   and possessing thee I have pleasure in nothing upon earth.
26 Though my flesh and my heart should have wasted away,
   God would for ever be the rock of my heart and my portion.

27 For behold, they that go afar from thee shall perish;
   every one that whores, falling from thee, dost thou extinguish.
28 But as for me, to be near to God is my happiness;
   I have put my trust in the Lord Jehovah
   that I may rehearse all thy works.

LXXIVe. WHY, O God, dost thou cast us off perpetually?
   why doth thine anger smoke against the sheep of thy pasture?
2 Remember thy congregation which thou gottest long since,
   which thou didst redeem as the tribe of thine inheritance;
   Mount Zion, whereon thou hast dwelt.
3 Lift up thy feet unto the perpetual ruins;
   the enemy hath marred all in the sanctuary.

4 Thy foes roared amid the place where thou didst meet us;
   they set up their signs for (true) signs.
5 They seemed like those who wield on high hatchets in a thicket of wood.
6 Then too its carved work altogether
   with axes and hammers they struck off.
7 They have set on fire thy sanctuary;
   they have profaned the dwelling-place of thy name to the ground.
8 They have said in their hearts, "Their family altogether!"
   they have burned up all God's places of meeting in the land.

9 We see not our signs, there is no prophet any more;
   neither is there with us any that knows how long.
10 How long, O God, shall the foe reproach?
   shall the enemy revile thy name perpetually?
11 Why withdrawest thou thy hand, even thy right hand?
   pluck it out of thy bosom, and make an end.

12 For God is my King from of old,
   who works salvation in the midst of the earth.
13 *Thou* didst divide the sea by thy strength;
   thou breakest the heads of the dragons on the waters.
14 *Thou* didst crush the heads of leviathan in pieces,
   and gavest him to be food for a people of wild beasts.
15 *Thou* didst cause fountain and torrent to break forth;
   thou didst dry up ever-flowing streams.

16 Thine is the day, thine also is the night;
   thou didst establish the light-bearer and the sun.
17 *Thou* didst set all the bounds of the earth;
   summer and winter—*thou* didst form them.

18 Remember how the enemy has reproached, Jehovah,
   and how a foolish people have reviled thy name.
19 Deliver not unto the sword the soul of thy turtle-dove;
   forget not the life of thine afflicted for ever.
20 Have regard to the covenant, for full are now become
   the dark places of the earth of haughtiness and violence.
21 O let not the down-trodden turn back ashamed;
   let the afflicted and the needy praise thy name.
22 Arise, O God, plead thy cause;
   remember how the fool reproaches thee all day long.
23 Forget not the voice of thy foes,
   the uproar of thine assailants which continually ascends.

LXXV. WE give thanks unto thee, O God, we give thanks unto thee;
   and they that call upon thy name rehearse thy wonders.

(God speaketh.)
2 For "I will seize the appointed time;
   I myself will judge in equity.

3 The earth and all its inhabitants melt with fear;
   I myself adjust the pillars of it.
4 I say unto the boasters, Be not so boastful,
   and to the ungodly, Do not exalt your horn;
5 Do not exalt your horn toward heaven,
   nor speak arrogantly with a stiff neck."

6 For not from the east, nor from the west,
   nor yet from the mountainous desert * * *
7 Nay, but God is the judge;
   this one he puts down, and that one he raises up.
8 For in the hand of Jehovah there is a cup with wine—
   foaming wine that is full of mixture;
   and he pours out of this into that,
   even the dregs thereof shall all the ungodly of the earth sup up and drink.

9 And as for me, I will declare it for ever;
   I will make melody unto the God of Jacob.
10 All the horns of the ungodly also will I cut off;
   exalted shall be the horns of the righteous.

LXXVIe. IN Judah is God renowned;
   his name is great in Israel.
2 For in Salem his bower was set,
   and his dwelling-place in Zion:
3 There brake he the lightnings of the bow,
   shield and sword, and equipment of war.

4 Fearful art thou; more glorious than the everlasting mountains.

5 Spoiled are the stout of heart, they sleep their slumber,
    and all the men of might have lost their hands.
6 At thy rebuke, O God of Jacob,
    a deep sleep fell both upon chariot and upon horse.

7 Thou! fearful art thou, and who can stand
    before thee when once thou art angry?
8 Out of heaven thou didst sound forth judgment;
    the earth feared and became still,
9 At God's rising up for judgment,
    to save all the afflicted of the land.

10 For the wrath of man shall give thanks unto thee;
    with the residue of (thy) great wrath thou wilt gird thyself.
11 Vow and pay unto Jehovah your God,
    let all around him bring presents,
12 Unto the Fearful One, who lops off the passion of princes,
    and is fearful to the kings of the earth.

LXXVIIe. "WITH my voice unto God fain would I cry,
    with my voice unto God, that he may hearken unto me."
2 In the day of my trouble (thus) did I seek the Lord;
    in the night was my hand stretched forth incessantly,
    my soul refused to be comforted.
3 "When I remember God, I can but moan;
    when I muse thereupon, my spirit faints away."

4 Thou didst hold open the guards of mine eyes;
  I was so stricken that I could not speak.
5 I considered the days of old,
  the years of ancient times:
6 "I will call to mind" (said I) "my song in the night,
  I will muse in my heart;" and my spirit (thus) searched out;
7 "Will the Lord cast off for ever,
  and be favourable no more?
8 Is his loving-kindness come utterly to an end?
  has his promise failed for all generations?
9 Has God forgotten to pity?
  or has he drawn in his compassions angrily?"

10 And I said, "It is my sickness:
  the years of the right hand of the most High!
11 I will celebrate the exploits of Jehovah,
  yea, remember thy wonders of old;
12 I will also meditate upon all thy work,
  and muse upon thy exploits."
13 O God, in holiness is thy way;
  who is so great a divinity as God?
14 Thou art the divinity that works marvels,
  thou hast made known among the peoples thy strength.
15 Thou hast guided thy people like sheep,
  the sons of Jacob and Joseph.

(Fragment of another Psalm.)

16 The waters saw thee, O God,
  the waters saw thee, and were in pangs;
  the abysses also trembled.

17 The clouds gushed out in water,
   the skies uttered a voice,
   thine arrows also went hither and thither.
18 The voice of thy thunder was in the whirlwind,
   flashes lightened the world,
   the earth trembled and quaked.
19 Through the sea went thy way,
   and thy path through great waters,
   and thy footprints could not be known.

LXXVIII. GIVE ear, O my people, to my teaching,
   incline your ear to the words of my mouth;
2 I would open my mouth in a parable,
   I would utter riddles of ancient date.
3 That which we have heard and known,
   and our fathers have rehearsed to us—
4 We will not hide from their children,
   rehearsing it to the generation to come,
   even the praises of Jehovah and his great force,
   and his wonderful works that he has done.

5 For he established a testimony in Jacob,
   and appointed a rule in Israel,
   which he commanded our fathers
   to make known to their children,
6 That the generation to come might know it,
   the children who should be born,
   who, rising up, might rehearse it to their children;

7 That they might place their confidence in God,
   and not forget the exploits of God,
   but keep his commandments,

8 And might not be as their fathers,
   an unruly and defiant generation,
   a generation that had not established their heart,
   and whose spirit was not faithful towards God.

9 The children of Ephraim, armed with the bow,
   turned back in the day of battle:
10 They kept not the covenant of God,
   and refused to walk in his law,
11 And forgot his exploits,
   and his wonders that he had shewed them.

12 Before their fathers he had done wonders,
   in the land of Egypt, the country of Zoan;
13 He clave the sea, and let them pass over,
   and piled up the waters as a harvest-heap;
14 And he guided them with a cloud by day,
   and all the night through with a light of fire.

15 He clave rocks in the wilderness,
    and gave them drink as from the ocean-floods
        abundantly;
16 And brought forth streams from the crag,
   and made the waters run down like rivers.
17 But they sinned yet more against him,
   defying the most High in the desert.

18 And they tempted God in their heart,
   requiring food for their lust;
19 And spake against God, and said,
   "Can God furnish a table in the wilderness?
20 Behold, he smote the rock, that the waters flowed
       forth,
   and torrents overflowed,
   can he give bread also,
   or provide flesh for his people?"

21 When he heard it, therefore, Jehovah was furious,
    and a fire was kindled against Jacob,
    and anger also came up against Israel ;
22 Because they believed not in God,
    and trusted not in his salvation.

23 And he commanded the clouds above,
    and opened the doors of heaven,
24 And rained upon them manna to eat,
    and gave them the corn of heaven.
25 Men did eat the food of the Mighty :
    he sent them provisions to the full.

26 He caused the east wind to set forth in heaven,
    and by his power he led on the south wind :
27 He rained flesh also upon them as dust,
    and winged birds as the sand of the sea ;
28 And let it fall within their camp,
    round about their dwellings.

29 So they did eat and were well filled,
    for that which they fancied he had brought unto them.
30 (But) not yet were they cloyed with their fancy,
    still was their food in their mouths,
31 When the anger of God came up against them,
    and slew the stoutest of them,
    and laid low the ripened youths of Israel.

32 For all this they sinned yet more,
    and believed not in his wondrous works.
33 So he made their days to vanish like a breath,
    and their years by a sudden end.
34 When he slew them, they inquired after him,
    and turned back, and sought God earnestly.

35 And they remembered that God was their rock,
    and God most High their redeemer,
36 But they only enticed him with their mouth.
    and lied unto him with their tongue;
37 Their heart was not stedfast towards him,
    neither were they faithful unto his covenant.

38 But he is full of compassion,
    forgives iniquity and destroys not;
    yea, many a time takes he back his anger,
    and arouses not all his wrath;
39 So he bethought him that they were but flesh,
    a wind that passes away, and comes not again.

40 How oft did they defy him in the wilderness,
    and pain him in the desert!
41 Yea, time after time they tempted God,
    and grieved the Holy One of Israel.
42 They remembered not his hand,
    the day when he set them free from the foe;
43 How he had set forth his signs in Egypt,
    and his wonders in the country of Zoan.

44 For he turned their Nile-canals into blood,
    and they could not drink their streams;
45 He sent among them dogflies, which devoured them,
    and frogs, which destroyed them.

46 He gave also their produce unto the caterpillar,
    and their labour unto the locust.
47 He killed their vines with hail,
    and their fig-trees with stones of ice,
48 And gave their cattle over to the hail,
    and their flocks to the (sky-sent) flames;

49 He sent against them his hot anger,
   fury, fervent ire, and trouble,
   as commissioned angels of woe.
50 He made a smooth road for his anger;
   he held not back their soul from death,
   but gave their life over to the pestilence.

51 And he smote every firstborn in Egypt,
   the firstlings of strength in the tents of Ham:
52 But he made his own people to go stage by stage like sheep,
   and led them on like a flock in the wilderness,
53 And guided them safely, that they were not affrighted,
   but the sea covered their enemies.

54 And he brought them unto his holy borders,
   to yon mount, which his own right hand had gotten;
55 And he drove out the nations before them,
   and those he allotted as a measured inheritance,
   and made the tribes of Israel to dwell in their tents.

56 But they tempted and defied God most High,
   and observed not his ordinances;
57 But swerved and were faithless like their fathers—
   turned aside like a deceitful bow,
58 For they vexed him with their high places,
   and moved him to jealousy with their graven images.

59 When God heard this, he was furious,
   and greatly abhorred Israel,

60 So that he cast off the dwelling-place of Shiloh,
   his tent where he had dwelt among men,
61 And delivered his own strength to captivity,
   and his splendour into the hand of the foe.

62 He abandoned his people to the sword,
   and was furious against his inheritance.
63 The fire devoured their young men,
   and their virgins were not praised in the song.
64 Their priests fell by the sword,
   and their widows could make no lamentation.

65 Then the Lord awaked as one that had slept,
   and like a mighty man that shouts from wine.
66 He beat his foes backward;
   he put upon them a perpetual reproach.
67 And he rejected the tent of Joseph,
   and chose not the tribe of Ephraim,
68 But chose the tribe of Judah,
   Mount Zion which he loved;
69 And he built his sanctuary like the heavenly heights,
   like the earth which he has founded for ever.

70 He chose David also his servant,
   and took him away from the sheepfolds;
71 From following the ewes he brought him,
   to feed Jacob his people and Israel his inheritance.
72 So he fed them according to the integrity of his heart,
   and with the skilfulness of his hands he guided them.

LXXIXe. O GOD, the heathen are come into thine inheritance;
they have defiled thy holy temple,
they have laid Jerusalem in ruins.
2 They have given the dead bodies of thy servants
as food unto the birds of the heaven,
the flesh of thy loving ones unto the wild beasts of the land.
3 They have shed their blood like water round about Jerusalem;
and there was none to bury them.
4 We are become a reproach to our neighbours,
a scorn and derision to them that are round about us.

5 How long, Jehovah, wilt thou be angry perpetually?
(how long) shall thy jealousy burn like fire?
6 Pour out thy wrath upon the nations that know thee not,
and upon the kingdoms that call not upon thy name.
7 For they have devoured Jacob,
and laid his homestead waste.
8 Remember not against us the iniquities of the ancestors;
let thy compassions quickly come to meet us,
for we are brought very low.

9 Help us, O God of our salvation, for the glory of thy name;
deliver us, and cancel our sins, for thy name's sake.

10 Wherefore should the nations say, Where is their
      God?
   let vengeance for the spilt blood of thy servants
      be shewed among the nations in our sight.
11 Let the groaning of the captive come before thee;
   according to the greatness of thine arm preserve
      thou the sons of death:
12 And pay back unto our neighbours sevenfold into
      their bosom
   their reproach wherewith they have reproached
      thee, O Lord.

13 So we that are thy people and the sheep of thy
      pasture
   will give thee thanks for ever,
   to many generations will we tell out thy praise.

LXXXc. 1a SHEPHERD of Israel, give ear,
         thou that leadest Joseph like a flock,
1b Inhabiter of the cherubim, shine forth
      before Ephraim and Benjamin and Manasseh,
2 Stir up thy heroic might,
      and come to our help!
3 Do thou, O God, restore us,
      cause thy face to shine, and we shall be saved.

4 Jehovah Sabáoth, how long
      hast thou smoked against the prayer of thy people!
5 Thou hast fed them with the bread of tears,
      and given them tears to drink in large measures.
6 Thou makest us a strife unto our neighbours,
      and our enemies make their game of us.
7 Jehovah Sabáoth, do thou restore us,
      cause thy face to shine, and we shall be saved.

8 Thou didst bring a vine out of Egypt;
   thou didst cast out the nations, and plant her in.
9 Thou didst clear a place before her;
   and when she had taken root she filled the land.
10 The mountains were covered with the shadow thereof,
   and the cedars of God with her branches.
11 She sent out her boughs even unto the sea,
   and her shoots unto the river.

14 Jehovah Sabáoth, do but look again
   from heaven, behold and give heed to this vine,
15 Even to the stock which thy right hand did plant,
   and to the leaves of the bough that thou didst choose thee.
12 Why hast thou broken down the fences thereof,
   so that all they that go by pluck off her grapes?
13 The boar out of the wood tears it,
   and the roamers of the plain feed off it.

16 Burned with fire is it, and cut down!
   at the rebuke of thy face let them perish!
17 Let thy hand be upon the man of thy right hand,
   upon the son of man whom thou didst choose thee.
18 [Deliver us] and we will not go back from thee;
   revive us, and we will call upon thy name.
19 Jehovah Sabáoth, do thou restore us;
   cause thy face to shine, and we shall be saved.

LXXXI. RING out your mirth unto God our strength;
   shout for joy unto the God of Jacob.
2 Swell the melody, and sound the timbrel,
   the pleasant lyre with the harp,

3 Blow the trumpet on the new moon,
   at the full moon, for our festal day.
4 For this is a statute for Israel,
   and an ordinance from the God of Jacob.
5 This he appointed in Joseph for a testimony,
   when he went forth over the land of Egypt.

*   *   *   *

(Fragment of another Psalm.)

*   *   *

the discourse of one I had not known did I hear.
6 "I removed his shoulder from the burden,
   his hands escaped from the basket.
7 Thou calledst in trouble, and I rescued thee,
   I answered thee in (my) thunder-covert,
   I proved thee at Meribah's waters.
8 (I said), Hear, O my people, and I will protest unto thee,
   O Israel, if thou wouldst but hearken unto me!
9 There shall no strange god be in thee,
   neither shalt thou worship any foreign god.
10 I am Jehovah thy God,
   who brought thee up out of the land of Egypt.
   Open thy mouth wide, and I will fill it.

11 But my people hearkened not unto my voice,
   and Israel was not compliant unto me.
12 So I let them go in the obstinacy of their heart,
   that they might walk in their own counsels.
13 O that my people were obedient unto me;
   that Israel would walk in my ways!
14 I would soon subdue their enemies,
   and turn my hand against their foes.

15 The haters of Jehovah should cringe unto them,
    that so their time might endure for ever;
16 And I would feed them with the fat of wheat,
    and with honey out of the rock would I satisfy thee."

LXXXIIe. GOD stands in a divine assembly;
    He judges amidst the gods.

2 " How long will ye judge unjustly,
    and accept the person of wicked men?
3 Redress the helpless and the orphan,
    justify the afflicted and the poor.
4 Deliver the helpless and needy;
    rid them out of the hand of the wicked."

5 " They are void of knowledge and understanding;
    they walk along in darkness;
    all the foundations of the earth are tottering.
6 I have said, Ye are gods,
    and ye are all the sons of the most High;
7 Nevertheless ye shall die like common men,
    and fall like any of the princes."

8 Arise, O God, judge the earth,
    for thou shalt possess thyself of all the nations.

LXXXIIIe. O GOD, be not silent,
    hush thee not, neither be still, O God.
2 For, lo, thine enemies make a roaring,
    and they that hate thee have lifted up the head:

3 They make a wily plot against thy people,
    and conspire against thy treasured ones:
4 They have said, Come, and let us extinguish them as a people,
    and let the name of Israel be mentioned no more.

5 For they have conspired with one accord,
    and are confederate against thee:
6 The tents of Edom and of the Ishmaelites,
    Moab and the Hagarenes;
7 Gebal, and Ammon, and Amalek,
    Philistia, with them that dwell at Tyre;
8 Asshur also has joined himself to them;
    they have been an arm to the children of Lot.

9 Deal with them as with Midian,
    as with Sisera, as with Jabin at the torrent of Kishon.
10 They were destroyed at Endor,
    they became as dung for the ground.
11 Make their nobles like Oreb and like Zeëb,
    and like Zebah and Zalmunna all their princes,
12 Who have said, " Let us take to ourselves
    The homesteads of God in possession."

13 My God, make them like unto whirling dust,
    and as the stubble before the wind;
14 As the fire that burns the forest,
    and as the flame that licks bare the mountains;
15 So pursue them with thy storm,
    and with thy hurricane confound them;
16 Fill their face with dishonour,
    that they may seek thy name, Jehovah.

17 Let them be put to shame and confounded for
 ever,
  yea, let them be abashed and perish,
18 That men may know that thou, even thou only,
  art the most High over all the earth.

LXXXIV. How lovely is thy dwelling-place,
   Jehovah Sabáoth !
2 My soul longs, yea, even pines
  for the courts of Jehovah ;
 My heart and my flesh ring out their joy
  unto the living God.

3 Even as the sparrow finds a house,
  and the swallow a nest,
 Where she lays her callow brood,
  [so have I found, even I,
 A home] by thine altars,
  O my King and my God.
4 Happy are they that dwell in thy house !
  they can be alway praising thee.

5 Happy the men whose strength is in thee,
  [who are pilgrims on] the highways
  [with gladness] in their heart !
6 When going through the balsam-vale,
  they make it a source of fountains ;
  yea, and the early rain mantles it with blessings:
7 They go from strength to strength,
  and shall appear before God in Zion.
8 Jehovah Sabáoth, hear thou my prayer ;
  give ear, O God of Jacob.

9 Behold, O God our shield,
   and regard the face of thine anointed.
10 For better is a day in thy courts
   than a thousand [spent abroad];
   I would choose to lie at the threshold in the
     house of my God,
   rather than to dwell in the tents of ungodliness.
11 For Jehovah, (even) God, is a sun and shield,
   Jehovah gives grace and glory;
   no good thing will he withhold
   from them that walk blamelessly.
12 Jehovah Sabáoth, happy is the man
   who trusts in thee!

LXXXV. JEHOVAH, thou hadst become favourable unto thy land,
   thou hadst turned the fortunes of Jacob:
2 Thou hadst forgiven the iniquity of thy people,
   thou hadst covered all their sin:
3 Thou hadst gathered in all thy fury,
   thou hadst turned from thy hot anger.

4 Return to us, O God of our salvation,
   and break to pieces thy grudge towards us.
5 Wilt thou be angry with us for ever?
   wilt thou stretch out thine anger unto all generations?
6 Wilt thou not revive us again,
   that thy people may rejoice in thee?
7 Make us to see thy lovingkindness, O God,
   and vouchsafe to grant us thy salvation.

8 Let me hear what God, yea, Jehovah, shall speak,
    surely he will speak peace to his people and to his
        loving ones,
    but let them not turn again to self-confidence.
9 Yea, near is his salvation to them that fear him,
    that glory may dwell in our land:
10 Lovingkindness and truth are met together,
    righteousness and peace have kissed each other:
11 Truth springs out of the earth,
    and righteousness looks down from heaven:
12 Jehovah shall give all that is good,
    and our land shall yield her increase.
13 [Righteousness shall walk before him,
    and shall give heed to the way of his steps.]

LXXXVI. INCLINE thine ear, Jehovah, and answer me,
    for I am afflicted and needy.
2 Preserve my soul, for I am one that loves,
    save thy servant, O thou my God,
    who trusts in thee.
3 Have pity on me, O Lord,
    for unto thee do I cry all the day.
4 Gladden the soul of thy servant,
    for unto thee, O Lord, do I lift up my soul.
5 For thou, Lord, art good and forgiving,
    and rich in lovingkindness to all that call upon
        thee.

6 Give ear, Jehovah, unto my prayer,
    and attend to the voice of my supplications.

7 In the day of my trouble I call upon thee,
    for thou wilt answer me.
8 There is none like thee among the gods, O Lord,
    and no works are like thine.
9 All nations whom thou hast made
    shall come and worship before thee, O Lord,
    and shall glorify thy name.
10 For thou art great and doest wondrous things,
    thou art God alone.

11 Teach me thy way, Jehovah, and I will walk in thy truthfulness:
    so shall my heart rejoice to fear thy name.
12 I will thank thee, O Lord my God, with all my heart,
    and glorify thy name for ever;
13 For great is thy lovingkindness towards me,
    and thou hast rescued my soul from the nether Hades.
14 O God, the proud have risen up against me,
    and a tyrannous crew have sought my soul,
    and have not set thee before them.
15 But thou, O Lord, art a God full of compassion and pity,
    longsuffering, and rich in lovingkindness and truth:
16 Turn thee unto me, and have pity upon me;
    give thy strength unto thy servant,
    and save the son of thy handmaid.
17 Work in my behalf some token for good,
    that they who hate me may see it and be ashamed,
    because thou, Jehovah, hast helped me and comforted me.

LXXXVIIᵉ. HIS foundation upon the holy mountains,
2 Yea, the gates of Zion Jehovah loves
   more than all the dwellings of Jacob.
3 Honourable things are spoken of thee,
   thou city of God.
4 "I will proclaim proud Egypt and Babylon to be
     my friends;
   behold Philistia and Tyre with Ethiopia—
   this one was born there."
5 And concerning Zion it shall be said,
   "This one and that one were born in her;"
   and he, the most High, shall stablish her.
6 Jehovah shall reckon, when he writes down the
     peoples,
   "This one was born there."
7 *   *   *
     *   *   *

LXXXVIIIᵉ. JEHOVAH my God, I have cried
     for help by day,
   and complained by night before thee;
2 O let my prayer come before thee,
   incline thine ear unto my piercing cry;

3 For my soul is sated with troubles,
   and my life has drawn near unto Hades.
4 I am counted with them that have gone down into
     the pit,
   I am become as a man that has no strength.

5 I am one turned adrift among the dead,
    like the slain that lie in the grave,
    whom thou rememberest no more,
    yea, they are severed from thy hand.

6 Thou hast laid me in the nether pit,
    in dark places and in gulfs;
7 Thy wrath rests upon me,
    and with all thy billows am I pressed down.

8 Thou hast removed my familiar friends far from me;
    thou hast made me an abomination unto them;
    I am shut in, so that I cannot come forth.
9 Mine eye pines away with affliction;
    Jehovah, I have called daily upon thee,
    I have spread open my hands unto thee.

10 Wilt thou perform wonders for the dead,
    or shall the shades arise and praise thee?
11 Shall thy lovingkindness be rehearsed in the grave,
    and thy faithfulness in Abaddon?
12 Shall thy wonders be made known in darkness,
    and thy righteousness in the land of oblivion?

13 And I—unto thee, Jehovah, do I cry,
    and at morn shall my prayer go to meet thee.
14 Why, Jehovah, castest thou off my soul,
    and hidest thy countenance from me?

15 I am afflicted and at my last breath even from youth;
    I bear thy terrors till my senses must fail:
16 Over me have passed thy fires of wrath,
    and thine alarms have extinguished me.

17 They have surrounded me, like water, all the day,
   they have hemmed me in together.
18 Thou hast put far from me lover and friend;
   as for my familiars—darkness!

LXXXIXe. I WILL sing of the lovingkindnesses of Jehovah for ever;
   with my mouth will I make known thy faithfulness to many generations.
2 For I say, "Lovingkindness will be built up for ever,
   in the heaven itself wilt thou establish thy faithfulness."

3 "I have made a covenant with my chosen one,
   I have sworn unto David my servant,
4 Thy seed will I establish for ever,
   and build up thy throne unto many generations."

5 And the heavens celebrate thy wonders, Jehovah,
   thy faithfulness also in the congregation of the holy ones.
6 For who in the sky shall rank with Jehovah,
   or be like unto Jehovah among the sons of God?

7 A God deeply to be revered in the council of holy ones,
   and to be had in awe of all that are round about him.
8 Jehovah, God of hosts,
   who is strong, Jehovah, like thee?
   *   *   *
   and thy faithfulness round about thee.

9 It is thou that rulest the insolence of the sea;
    when its billows roar, it is thou that stillest them:
10 Thou that didst crush proud Egypt as one that is slain,
    with thy strong arm thou didst scatter thine enemies:

11 Thine are the heavens, thine also is the earth;
    the world and its fulness—*thou* didst found them.
12 The north and the south—*thou* didst create them,
    Tabor and Hermon ring out their joy at thy name.

13 Thine is an arm with heroic might;
    strong is thy hand, high is thy right hand.
14 Righteousness and justice are the base of thy throne,
    lovingkindness and truth go to meet thy presence.

15 Happy the people that know the glad shouting,
    that walk, O Jehovah, in the light of thy countenance!
16 In thy name do they exult all the day long,
    and through thy righteousness are they exalted.

17 For thou art the glory of their strength,
    and in thy favour thou exaltest our horn.
18 For to Jehovah belongs our shield,
    yea, our king to the Holy One of Israel.

19 There was a time when thou spakest in a vision
    unto thy loving one, and saidst,
    "I have laid strength upon a mighty man,
    I have exalted one chosen out of the people.

20 I have found David my servant,
   with my holy oil have I anointed him;
21 By whose side shall be my hand unmoveably,
   mine arm also shall strengthen him.

22 No enemy shall oppress him as a creditor,
   nor any son of injustice afflict him;
23 But I will shatter his foes before him,
   and smite them that hate him;

24 And my faithfulness and lovingkindness shall be with him,
   and through my name shall his horn be exalted;
25 I will make his hand reach to the sea,
   and his right hand to the streams.

26 He shall call upon me, Thou art my father,
   my God, and the rock of my salvation;
27 I also will appoint him to be firstborn,
   the most High to the kings of the earth.

28 I will keep for him for ever my lovingkindness,
   and my covenant shall be unfailing towards him;
29 And I will make his seed imperishable,
   and his throne as the days of heaven.

30 If his children forsake my law,
   and walk not in mine ordinances,
31 If they profane my statutes,
   and keep not my commandments;

32 I will visit their transgression with the rod,
   and their iniquity with scourges:

33 But my lovingkindness I will not withdraw from him,
　　Neither will I belie my faithfulness;

34 My covenant I will not profane,
　　nor alter the thing that is gone out of my lips;
35 I have sworn once by my holiness,
　　Verily I will not be false to David;

36 His seed shall endure for ever,
　　and his throne as the sun before me:
37 As the moon, it shall be stedfast for ever;
　　and the witness in the sky is faithful."

38 But thou—thou hast cast off and spurned,
　　and hast become furious against thine anointed.
39 Thou hast abhorred the covenant of thy servant,
　　thou hast profaned his crown to the ground.

40 Thou hast broken down all his fences,
　　thou hast made his citadels a ruin;
41 All that pass by the way spoil him,
　　he is become a reproach to his neighbours.

42 Thou hast exalted the right hand of his foes,
　　thou hast made all his enemies to rejoice;
43 Thou didst also turn back the edge of his sword,
　　and didst not cause him to stand in the battle.

44 Thou hast put an end to his lustre,
　　and hast hurled his throne to the ground;
45 Thou hast shortened the days of his youth,
　　thou hast wrapped him with shame.

46 How long, Jehovah, wilt thou hide thyself perpetually?
   (how long) shall thy wrath burn like fire?
47 Remember how short my time is,
   for what vanity thou hast created all the children of men!

48 Who is the man that shall live on and not see death,
   or win escape for his soul from the hand of Hades?
49 Lord, where are thy old lovingkindnesses
   which thou swarest unto David in thy faithfulness?

50 Remember, Lord, the reproach of thy servants,
   how I bear in my bosom the reproach of peoples;
51 Wherewith thine enemies, Jehovah, have reproached,
   wherewith they have reproached the footsteps of thine anointed.

(Subscription to Book III.)

52 Blessed be Jehovah for evermore!
   Amen and Amen.

BOOK IV.

PSALM XC.

LORD, thou hast been unto us an asylum from age to age.
2 Before the mountains were born,
    or the earth and the world were brought forth,
    yea, from æon to æon thou art God.
3 Thou turnest mortals back to dust,
    and sayest, "Return, ye sons of the earth-born."
4 For a thousand years are in thine eyes
    as yesterday when it is passing,
    and a watch in the night.

5 Thou floodest them away; they become as a sleep;
    in the morning they are as grass which sprouts again;
6 In the morning it blossoms and sprouts again,
    in the evening it is cut down and withers.
7 For we are wasted away through thine anger,
    and through thy wrath have we been confounded.
8 Thou hast set our iniquities before thee,
    those that none can discern in the shining of thy countenance.

9 For our days have all died away as a murmur,
   through thy fury have we now finished our years.
10 The days of our years are threescore years and ten,
   and if we are of full strength, then fourscore;
   and their proud boasting is travail and vanity,
   so quickly is it gone by, and we take our flight.
11 (But) who hath learned the strength of thine anger,
   and, according to the fear of thee, thy fury?
12 Thus learn us to number our days,
   and we shall take home wisdom to our heart.

13 Return, Jehovah, how long?
   and relent over thy servants.
14 Satisfy us with thy lovingkindness in the morning,
   and we will give ringing shouts of joy all our days:
15 Make us to rejoice according to the days thou hast afflicted us,
   the years wherein we have seen adversity.
16 Let thy doing be manifest to thy servants.
   and thy majesty unto their children;
17 And let the pleasantness of Jehovah our God brood over us,
   and the work of our hands O prosper thou over us,
   yea, prosper thou our handiwork.

XCI^e. [HAPPY] he that sits in the covert of the most High,
   that abides under the shadow of the Almighty,
2 That says unto Jehovah, My refuge and my fortress,
   my God, in whom I trust.

3 For he shall rescue thee from the snare of the fowler,
   from the destroying pestilence.
4 With his pinions shall he screen thee,
   and under his wings shalt thou find refuge;
   shield and targe shall be his truth.

5 Thou shalt not be afraid for the terror of the night,
   for the arrow that flies by day;
6 For the plague that advances in darkness,
   for the pestilence that spoils at noonday.
7 A thousand may fall beside thee,
   and ten thousand at thy right hand;
   it shall not approach thee.
8 Only with thine eyes shalt thou look on,
   and see the recompence of the wicked.

9 Because thou hast said, "Jehovah is my refuge,"
   and hast made the most High thine asylum,
10 No evil shall be sent to meet thee,
   no scourge shall come nigh thy tent.
11 For he shall give his angels charge concerning thee
   to keep thee in all thy ways.
12 Upon their hands shall they bear thee,
   lest thou strike thy foot against a stone.
13 Thou shalt tread upon lion and adder,
   upon young lion and dragon shalt thou trample.

14 Because he hath fixed his love upon me, therefore will I rescue him;
   I will set him secure, because he knows my name.
15 When he calls upon me, I will answer him;
   I will be with him in trouble;
   I will deliver him, and bring him to honour.

16 With length of days will I satisfy him,
   and feast his eyes with my salvation.

XCII. Good is it to give thanks unto Jehovah,
   and to make melody unto thy name,
   O most High,
2 To publish thy lovingkindness in the morning,
   and thy faithfulness in the night seasons,
3 With a ten-stringed instrument, yea, with the harp,
   with sounding music upon the lyre.

4 For thou hast gladdened me, Jehovah, with thine operation;
   I will ring out my joy in the works of thy hands.
5 How great are thy works, Jehovah!
   very deep are thy designs.

6 A brutish man discerns it not,
   neither can a fool understand this.
7 When the ungodly sprung up as the herbage,
   and all the workers of naughtiness blossomed,
   it was that they might be destroyed for ever;
8 But thou, Jehovah, art in the high heaven for evermore.

9 For lo, thine enemies, Jehovah, shall perish;
   all the workers of naughtiness shall be scattered abroad:
10 But thou hast exalted my horn as that of a wild ox,
   my wasting strength with fresh oil:
11 Mine eye also has looked its full upon mine adversaries,
   upon them that rose up against me, doers of evil.

12 The righteous shall spring up like a palm-tree,
   and grow tall as a cedar in Lebanon.
13 Planted in the house of Jehovah,
   they shall flourish in the courts of our God.
14 They shall still shoot forth in old age,
   fat shall they be, and fresh,
15 To declare that Jehovah is upright,
   that in my Rock there is no unrighteousness.

XCIII. JEHOVAH is become king, he hath robed him in majesty,
he hath robed him, yea, he has girt him with strength;
stablished therefore is the world, tottering not.
2 Stablished is thy throne from of old;
   thou art from everlasting.

3 The streams have lifted up, Jehovah,
   the streams have lifted up their voice;
   the streams lift up their din.

4 Than the voices of many waters,
   glorious waters, breakers of ocean,
   more glorious in the height is Jehovah.

5 Thy testimonies are very faithful;
   holiness is seemly for thy house
   unto length of days.

XCIV. O GOD of vengeances, Jehovah,
O God of vengeances, shine forth:
2 Lift up thyself, O Judge of the earth,
render their deserts to the proud.

3 Jehovah, how long shall the ungodly,
how long shall the ungodly triumph?
4 They belch out, they utter arrogant things,
they carry themselves high—all the workers of naughtiness.

5 They crush thy people, Jehovah,
and afflict thy heritage;
6 The widow and the sojourner they slay,
and the orphans they murder;

7 And they say, "Jah will not see,
neither will the God of Jacob regard it.
8 Take heed, ye brutish among the people,
and O ye fools, when will ye deal wisely?

9 He that planted the ear, shall he not hear?
or he that formed the eye, shall he not look?
10 He that chastises the nations, shall he not punish?
he that teaches man knowledge?
11 Jehovah knows the schemes of man,
that they are but a breath.

12 Happy the man whom thou admonishest, Jah,
and teachest out of thy law,

13 To give him rest from the days of adversity,
   until the pit be digged for the ungodly!

14 For Jehovah will not abandon his people,
   neither will he forsake his inheritance,
15 For judgment must turn again to righteousness,
   and all the upright in heart follow it.

16 Who will rise up for me against the evil-doers?
   who will set himself on my side against the workers of naughtiness?
17 Unless Jehovah had been my help,
   my soul had soon dwelt in Silence.

18 When I say, " My foot fails,"
   thy lovingkindness, Jehovah, holds me up.
19 When my distracted thoughts crowd within me,
   thy consolations delight my soul.

20 Can such be allied with thee—the tribunal of destruction,
   which frames mischief according to law?
21 They attack the soul of the righteous,
   and condemn the innocent blood.

22 Therefore Jehovah shall be unto me a sure retreat,
   and my God the rock of my refuge.
23 He shall bring back upon them their own wickedness,
   and quiet them for ever for their malice,
   Jehovah our God shall quiet them for ever.

XCVe. COME, let our cries ring unto Jehovah,
　　　　let us shout unto the rock of our salvation.
2 Let us go to meet his presence with thanksgiving,
　　let us shout unto him with chantings.
3 For Jehovah is a great God,
　　and a great King above all gods :
4 In whose hand are the recesses of the earth,
　　and the summits of the mountains are his ;
5 Whose is the sea, and he made it,
　　and his hands formed the dry land.
6 Come, let us worship and bow down,
　　let us kneel before Jehovah our maker :
7 For he is our God, and we—
　　the people of his hand and the sheep of his pasture.

*　　*　　*　　*　　*　　*

(Fragment of another Psalm.)

*　　*　　*　　to-day !
　oh that ye would hear his voice !
8 Harden not your heart, as at Meribah,
　　as in the day of Massah in the wilderness,
9 Where your fathers tried me,
　　proved me, but also saw my work.
10 For forty years I had a loathing at this generation,
　　and said, "They are a people that go astray in their heart,
　　and ignorant are they of my ways ; "
11 So that I sware in mine anger,
　　Surely they shall not enter into my rest.

XCVI^e. SING unto Jehovah a new song,
     sing unto Jehovah, all the earth.
2 Sing unto Jehovah, bless his name;
     tell the news of his salvation from day to day.
3 Rehearse his glory among the nations,
     his wonders among all peoples.

4 For great is Jehovah, and highly to be praised,
     terrible is he above all gods:
5 For all the gods of the nations are but vain gods,
     but it is Jehovah that made the heavens:
6 Glory and grandeur are before him;
     strength and splendour are in his sanctuary.

7 Ascribe unto Jehovah, O ye families of the peoples,
     ascribe unto Jehovah glory and strength:
8 Ascribe unto Jehovah the glory of his name,
     take offerings, and come into his courts.
9 Worship Jehovah in hallowed pomp,
     be in pangs before him, all the earth.

10 Utter it among the nations, "Jehovah has become King,"
     stablished therefore is the world, tottering not;
     he shall give doom to the peoples in equity.
11 Let the heavens rejoice, and let the earth exult,
     let the sea thunder and the fulness thereof;

12 Let the plain triumph and all that is in it,
     moreover, let all the trees of the forest give a ringing cry

13 Before Jehovah, for he comes
    for he comes to judge the earth;
    he will judge the world in righteousness,
    and the peoples in his faithfulness.

XCVII^e. JEHOVAH has become King, let the earth exult,
    let many far-off lands rejoice;
2 Clouds and darkness are round about him,
    righteousness and justice are the base of his throne:
3 Fire goes before him,
    and licks up his foes round about.
4 His lightnings give shine unto the world,
    the earth sees it, and is in pangs:
5 The mountains melt like wax before Jehovah,
    before the Lord of the whole earth:
6 The heavens declare his righteousness,
    and all the peoples have seen his glory.

8 Zion hears it and rejoices,
    and the daughters of Judah exult,
    because of thy judgments, Jehovah.
7 Shamed are all they that serve graven images,
    that make their boast of vain gods;
    worship him, all ye gods!
9 For thou, Jehovah, art most High above all the earth,
    greatly exalted above all gods.

10 O friends of Jehovah, hate the evil thing,
        *   *   *   *
    he preserves the souls of his loving ones,
    from the hand of the ungodly he delivers them.

11 Light arises for the righteous,
    and joy for the upright in heart:
12 Rejoice, ye righteous, in Jehovah,
    and give thanks to his holy memorial.

XCVIII. SING ye unto Jehovah a new song,
    for marvellous things has he done;
his own right hand has helped him,
and his holy arm.
2 His saving help Jehovah has made known;
    before the eyes of the nations
    has he unveiled his righteousness.
3 His kindness and faithfulness has he remembered
    unto the house of Israel;
all the ends of the world have seen
the saving help of our God.

4 Shout merrily unto Jehovah, all ye upon earth,
    break into a ringing cry, and make melody:
5 Make melody unto Jehovah with the lyre,
    with the lyre and the sound of melody:
6 With trumpets and sound of cornet,
    shout before the King Jehovah.
7 Let the sea thunder and the fulness thereof,
    the world and they that dwell therein:
8 Let the streams clap their hands,
    let the mountains together give a ringing cry
9 Before Jehovah, for he comes to judge the earth,
    he shall judge the world with righteousness,
    and the peoples in equity.

XCIX. JEHOVAH has become King; the peoples
must tremble:
he inhabits the cherubim, the earth must quiver.
2 Jehovah is great in Zion,
and high is he over all the peoples.
3 They shall give thanks unto thy name so great and
fearful,
he is the Holy One.

4 And the strength of a king that loves justice
thou thyself hast established in equity;
justice and righteousness thou thyself hast wrought
in Jacob.
5 Exalt ye Jehovah our God,
and worship at his footstool;
he is the Holy One.

6 Moses and Aaron among his priests,
and Samuel among those that called upon his
name—
called upon Jehovah and he answered them.
7 In a pillar of cloud he spake unto them,—
they had observed his testimonies and the statute
he had given them.
8 Thou answeredst them, Jehovah our God,
a pardoning God wast thou unto them,
but one that took vengeance for their misdeeds.
9 Exalt ye Jehovah our God,
and worship at his holy mountain,
for Jehovah our God is the Holy One.

C. SHOUT merrily unto Jehovah, all ye upon earth:
2 Serve Jehovah with gladness,
    come before him with ringing cries.
3 Be sure that Jehovah is God;
    he made us, and his are we,
    even his people and the sheep of his pasture.
4 Enter his gates with thanksgiving,
    and his courts with praise;
    give thanks unto him, bless his name.
5 For gracious is Jehovah, his kindness is everlasting,
    and from generation to generation his faithfulness.

CI. OF lovingkindness and justice would I sing,
    Unto thee, Jehovah, would I make melody.
2 I would take heed to the way of perfectness;
    (when wilt thou come unto me?)
    I will walk in the perfectness of my heart
    within my house.
3 I will not set before mine eyes
    any villainous thing;
    deeds that swerve do I hate—
    such shall not cleave unto me.
4 A perverse heart shall depart from me;
    evil I will not know.
5 Whoso secretly slanders his neighbour,
    him will I quiet for ever:
    him that has high looks and a swollen heart
    I cannot endure.

6 Mine eyes are upon the faithful of the land,
   that they may dwell with me;
   whoso walks in the way of perfectness,
   he shall minister unto me;
7 None shall dwell within my house
   that practises guile;
   he that tells lies shall have no station
   where I may see.
8 Each morn will I quiet for ever
   all the ungodly of the land,
   that I may cut off from the city of Jehovah
   all that work naughtiness.

CII^e. JEHOVAH, hear my prayer,
   and let my cry come unto thee.
2 Hide not thy face from me in the day of my straits,
   incline thine ear unto me;
   in the day that I call answer me speedily.

3 For my days have vanished like smoke,
   and my bones are burned through like a hearth.
4 My heart is smitten like the herbage, and dried up;
   in truth, I have forgotten to eat my bread.
5 For the sound of my sighing my bones
   cleave [to my skin and] to my flesh.

6 I am like a pelican of the wilderness,
   I am become as an owl of the ruins:
7 I am sleepless and must moan aloud
   like a solitary bird upon the roof:
8 Mine enemies reproach me all the day long,
   they that are frantic against me curse by my name.

9 For I have eaten ashes like bread,
 and mingled my drink with tears,
10 Because of thy fervent ire and indignation,
 for thou hast lifted me up and cast me away.
11 My days are like a stretched-out shadow,
 yea, as for me, I am becoming dry as the herbage.

12 But thou, Jehovah,—thou art seated for ever,
 and thy fame endures unto all generations;
13 Thou wilt arise and have compassion upon Zion,
 for it is time to have pity on her, for the set time
   is come:
14 For thy servants take pleasure in her stones,
 and it pities them to see her in the dust.

15 The nations also shall fear Jehovah's name,
 and all the kings of the earth thy glory,
16 Because Jehovah has built up Zion,
 and has shown himself in his glory,
17 Has turned toward the prayer of the destitute,
 and not despised their prayer.

18 Recorded shall this be for the next generation,
 and the people to be created shall praise Jah,
19 Because he has looked down from his holy height,
 out of heaven has Jehovah gazed upon the earth,
20 To hear the groaning of the captive,
 to loose the sons of death,
21 That they may rehearse the name of Jehovah in
   Zion,
 and his praise in Jerusalem;
22 When the peoples are gathered together,
 the kingdoms also to serve Jehovah.

23 He has brought down my strength in the way,
   he has shortened my days:
24 I will say, My God, take me not away
   in the midst of my days,
   thou whose years endure throughout all ages.
25 Of old thou didst lay the foundations of the earth,
   and the heavens are the work of thy hands.
26 They shall perish, but thou shalt continue,
   and they all shall wax old as a garment:
   as a robe shalt thou change them, and they shall
      be changed,
27 But thou art the same,
   and thy years shall have no end.
28 The children of thy servants shall abide,
   and their seed shall be established before thee.

CIII. MY soul, bless Jehovah,
   and all that is within me (bless) his
      holy name.
2 My soul, bless Jehovah,
   and forget not all his benefits;
3 Who forgives all thine iniquities,
   and heals all thy sicknesses;
4 Who releases thy life from the pit,
   and crowns thee with kindness and tender mercies:
5 Who satisfies thy mouth with good things,
   so that thy youth is renewed as the eagle's.

6 Jehovah executes righteous acts,
   and judgments for all that are oppressed.
7 He made known his ways unto Moses,
   his exploits unto the children of Israel.

8 Jehovah is full of compassion and pity,
   long-suffering, and plenteous in lovingkindness:
9 He will not contend perpetually,
   nor keep his anger for ever.
10 He has not dealt with us after our sins,
   nor requited us according to our iniquities.

11 For as the heaven is high above the earth,
   so mighty is his kindness over them that fear him;
12 As far as sunrise from sunset
   he has removed our transgressions from us.
13 As a father has compassion upon his sons,
   Jehovah has compassion upon them that fear him.
14 For he—he knows our frame,
   and bethinks him that we are dust.

15 Mortal man, his days are as grass,
   as a flower of the field, so he blossoms;
16 For a wind passes over it, and it is gone,
   and its place knows it no more.
17 But the kindness of Jehovah is from æon to æon
      brooding over them that fear him,
   and his righteousness is unto children's children,
18 To such as keep his covenant,
   and remember his behests to do them.

19 Jehovah has established his throne in heaven,
   and his dominion rules over all.
20 Bless Jehovah, ye angels of his,
   ye mighty in power, that perform his word:
21 Bless Jehovah, all ye his hosts,
   ye ministers of his, that perform his will:
22 Bless Jehovah, all his works,
   in all places of his dominion.
   My soul, bless Jehovah!

CIV MY soul, bless Jehovah!
O Jehovah my God, thou art very great,
thou hast robed thee in glory and grandeur.
2 He wraps himself in light as in a mantle,
he stretches out the heavens like a tent-curtain;
3 He lays the beams of his upper-chambers in the waters,
he makes the clouds his chariot,
he travels upon the wings of the wind;
4 He makes his messengers of winds,
his ministers of fire and flame.

5 He founded the earth upon its bases,
that it might be unshaken for ever and ever:
6 With the flood as with a robe thou coveredst it,
waters stood above the mountains.
7 At thy rebuke they fled,
at the voice of thy thunder they were scared away—
8 The mountains rose, the valleys sank—
unto the place which thou hadst founded for them.
9 Thou didst appoint a bound, that they might not pass over,
nor turn again to cover the earth.

10 He sends forth springs into the ravines,
between the mountains do they make their course:
11 They give drink to every beast of the plain,
the wild asses quench their thirst:
12 Over them dwell the birds of the heaven,
from among the branches do they sing.

13 To the mountains he gives drink from his upper
    chambers,
    the earth hath its fill by the fruit of thy works.

14 He causes grass to spring up for the cattle,
    herbs also for the service of men;
15 To bring forth bread from the earth,
    and that wine may gladden weak man's heart;
    to make his face shine with oil,
    and that bread may sustain weak man's heart.
16 The trees of Jehovah have their fill,
    the cedars of Lebanon which he planted,
17 Wherein the birds make their nests;
    the stork—her house is in the fir-trees:
18 The high mountains are for the wild goats,
    the rocks are a refuge for the badgers.

19 He made the moon for solemn seasons;
    the sun knows his going down.
20 Wilt thou have darkness? straightway it is night,
    wherein all the beasts of the forest do move:
21 The young lions roar after their prey,
    and seek their food from God:
22 When the sun arises, they withdraw themselves,
    and lay them down in their dens.
23 Man goes forth to his work
    and to his labour until the evening.

24 How manifold are thy works, Jehovah!
    in wisdom hast thou made them all;
    the earth is full of thy creatures.
25 Yonder sea, so great, and stretching on either hand—
    therein are things moving innumerable,
    living creatures both small and great;

26 There do the ships make their course,
    there is Leviathan whom thou didst form to sport with him.
27 All wait upon thee,
    that their food may be given them in due season.
28 Thou givest to them—they gather;
    thou openest thy hand—they are filled with good.
29 Thou hidest thy face—they are confounded;
    thou withdrawest their breath—they gasp,
    and turn again to their dust.
30 Thou sendest forth thy breath—they are created,
    and thou renewest the face of the earth.

31 Let the glory of Jehovah endure for ever!
    let Jehovah rejoice in his works!
32 (The God) who looks upon the earth, and it trembles;
    if he touch the mountains, they smoke.
33 I would sing unto Jehovah while I live,
    make melody unto my God, while I have my being.
34 Pleasant be my musing unto him;
    as for me, I will rejoice in Jehovah.
35 Let the sinners be consumed out of the earth,
    and the ungodly, let them vanish away.
    My soul, bless Jehovah!
        Hallelujah.

CV^e. O GIVE thanks unto Jehovah, celebrate his name,
    spread abroad his exploits among the peoples.

2 Sing unto him, make melody unto him,
   discourse ye of all his wondrous works.
3 Let your glorying be in his holy name;
   let the heart of them rejoice that seek Jehovah.
4 Inquire after Jehovah and his strength,
   be seeking his face continually.
5 Remember his wonders that he has done,
   his prodigies and the judgments of his mouth,
6 O ye seed of Abraham his servant,
   ye children of Jacob his chosen.

7 He, Jehovah, is our God,
   his judgments are in all the earth:
8 He remembers his covenant for ever,
   the word which he appointed for a thousand
       generations,
9 That which he made with Abraham,
   his oath also unto Isaac,
10 And which he confirmed unto Jacob for a statute,
   and to Israel for an everlasting covenant,
11 Saying, "Unto thee will I give the land of Canaan,
   to be your measured inheritance."

12 While they were still easily numbered,
   very few, and sojourners in the land,
13 And went about from nation to nation,
   from one kingdom to another people,
14 He suffered no man to oppress them,
   and punished kings for their sakes,
15 (Saying,) Touch not mine anointed ones,
   and do my prophets no harm.

16 And he summoned a famine on the land,
   he brake the whole staff of bread:

17 He sent a man before them,
   Joseph was sold to be a bondservant:
18 They galled his feet with fetters,
   his soul went into the iron:
19 Until the time that his word came to pass,
   when the promise of Jehovah had assayed him.
20 The king sent and loosed him,
   the ruler of peoples, and let him go free.
21 He made him lord over his house,
   and ruler of all his possessions,
22 To bind his princes at pleasure,
   and to make his elders wise.

23 So Israel came into Egypt,
   and Jacob was a sojourner in the land of Ham;
24 And he increased his people exceedingly,
   and made them stronger than their foes.
25 He turned their heart to hate his people,
   to deal craftily with his servants.
26 He sent Moses his servant,
   and Aaron whom he had chosen.
27 He set forth his signs among them,
   and prodigies in the land of Ham.

28 He sent darkness, and it grew dark,
   and yet they rebelled against his words.
29 He turned their waters into blood,
   and slew their fish.
30 Their land swarmed with frogs,
   they came up into their kings' chambers.
31 He spake and the beetles came,
   and gnats in all their borders.
32 For rains he gave them hail,
   fiery flames in their land.

33 He smote their vines also and their fig-trees,
    and brake in pieces the trees of their borders.
34 He spake, and the locusts came,
    and caterpillars without number,
35 And ate up every herb in their land,
    and ate up the fruit of their ground.
36 He smote also every first-born in their land,
    the firstlings of all their strength;
37 But those he brought out with silver and gold,
    there was not one feeble person among his tribes.

38 Egypt rejoiced at their departing,
    for their terror had fallen upon them.
39 He spread out clouds for a covering,
    and fire to illumine the night.
40 They asked, and he brought quails,
    and satisfied them with the bread of heaven.
41 He opened the rock and waters gushed out,
    they coursed through the desert as a river.
42 For he remembered his holy promise,
    and Abraham his servant;
43 And brought forth his people with joy,
    his chosen ones with ringing cries;
44 And gave them the lands of the nations,
    and they inherited the toil of the peoples,
45 In order that they might keep his statutes,
    and observe his laws.
        Hallelujah.

CVI.

HALLELUJAH.
O give thanks unto Jehovah, for he is good,
for his mercy endures for ever.
2 Who can express the mighty acts of Jehovah,
and show forth all his praise?
3 Happy are they that observe right,
and do righteousness at all times.
4 Remember me, Jehovah, with thy favour for thy people,
visit me with thy salvation;
5 That I may look on the good fortune of thy chosen,
may rejoice in the joy of thy nation,
may glory with thine inheritance.

6 We have sinned with our fathers,
we have done perversely, wickedly.
7 Our fathers heeded not thy wonders in Egypt,
remembered not thine abundant lovingkindnesses,
but were defiant at the sea, even by the Red Sea.
8 Yet he saved them for his name's sake
to make his might to be known.
9 For he rebuked the Red Sea, and it became dry,
and he led them through the floods as through the wilderness;
10 And saved them from the hand of the malicious,
and released them from the hand of the enemy.
11 The waters covered their foes;
not one of them remained.
12 Then believed they his words;
they sang his praise.

13 Soon they forgot his works;
   they did not wait for his purpose;
14 But lusted a lust in the wilderness,
   and tempted God in the desert;
15 And he gave them their request,
   but despatched leanness against their soul.
16 They envied Moses also in the camp,
   and Aaron the saint of Jehovah:
17 The earth opened, and swallowed up Dathan,
   and covered the company of Abiram;
18 And fire kindled on their company,
   the flame licked up the ungodly.
19 They made a calf at Horeb,
   and worshipped a molten image.
20 Thus they exchanged his glory
   for the image of an ox that eateth herbage.
21 They forgot God their saviour,
   who had done great things in Egypt,
22 Wondrous things in the land of Ham,
   fearful things by the Red Sea;
23 And he said he would exterminate them,
   but Moses his chosen [rose],
   and stood in the breach before him,
   to turn away his wrath, that he might not destroy.

24 They held the desirable land for nought,
   they believed not his word,
25 And murmured in their tents,
   hearkening not unto the voice of Jehovah.
26 So he lifted up his hand against them
   to cut them down in the wilderness;
27 To scatter their seed among the nations,
   and to winnow them in the lands.

28 They yoked themselves also unto Baal-peor,
    and ate the sacrifices of the dead,
29 And vexed (Jehovah) by their doings,
    and a plague broke in upon them.
30 Then stood up Phinehas and interposed,
    and so the plague was stayed;
31 And that was counted unto him for righteousness
    unto all generations for evermore.
32 And they stirred up indignation at the waters of Meribah,
    and it went ill with Moses on their account;
33 For they had been defiant towards God's spirit,
    and he spoke unadvisedly with his lips.

34 They did not exterminate the nations,
    concerning whom Jehovah had commanded them,
35 But mingled themselves among the nations,
    and learned their works;
36 And they served their idols,
    and these became a snare unto them,
37 For they sacrificed their sons,
    their daughters also, to the demons,
38 And shed innocent blood,
    the blood of their sons and of their daughters,
    whom they sacrificed to the idols of Canaan,
    so that the land was profaned with bloodshed;
39 And they became unclean through their works,
    and committed whoredom by their misdeeds.
40 Then did the anger of Jehovah burn against his people,
    insomuch that he abhorred his inheritance;
41 And he gave them into the hand of the nations,
    and they that hated them ruled over them.

42 Their enemies oppressed them,
   and they were made subject to their hand.
43 Many times did he deliver them,
   but they clung defiantly to their own purpose,
   and pined away for their iniquity.

44 But he looked on their adversity,
   when he heard their cry,
45 And remembered for them his covenant,
   and relented according to his plenteous kindness,
46 And caused them to get compassion
   from all those that carried them captives.

47 Save us, Jehovah our God,
   and gather us from among the nations
   to give thanks unto thy holy name,
   to make our boast of thy praises.

(Subscription to Book IV.)

48 Blessed be Jehovah, Israel's God,
   from æon to æon;
   and let all the people say, Amen.
      Hallelujah.

BOOK V.

PSALM CVII.[e]

O GIVE thanks unto Jehovah, for he is good,
    for his mercy endures for ever.
2 Thus let the released of Jehovah say,
    whom he hath released from the hand of the foe,
3 And gathered out of the lands,
    from the east and from the west,
    from the north and from the south.

4 They wandered in the wilderness, yea, in the desert,
    they found no road to a city of habitation:
5 Hungry and thirsty,
    their soul fainted in them.
6 So they cried unto Jehovah in their strait,
    and he delivered them out of their distresses,
7 He directed them also by a straight way,
    that they might go to a city of habitation.
8 O let these give thanks unto Jehovah for his kindness,
    and for his wondrous works to the children of men!

9 For he has satisfied the longing soul,
   and filled the hungry soul with good.

10 Those that sat in darkness and in deadly shade,
   bondsmen of affliction and iron—
11 Because they defied the commands of God,
   and reviled the purpose of the most High,
12 So that he bowed their heart down with travail,
   they stumbled, and there was none to help,
13 But they cried unto Jehovah in their strait,
   and he saved them out of their distresses,
14 Brought them out of darkness and deadly shade,
   and tore away their bonds—
15 O let these give thanks unto Jehovah for his kindness,
   and for his wondrous works to the children of men!
16 For he has broken the gates of brass,
   and hewed the bars of iron in sunder.

17 Sick men, who for the way of their transgression
   and for their iniquities suffered affliction—
18 Their soul abhorred all manner of food,
   and they drew nigh unto the gates of Death,
19 But they cried unto Jehovah in their strait,
   and he saved them out of their distresses,
20 He sent his word to heal them,
   and caused them to escape from their pitfalls—
21 O let these give thanks unto Jehovah for his kindness,
   and for his wondrous works to the children of men,
22 And offer the sacrifices of thanksgiving,
   and tell out his works amid cries that ring.

23 They that go down upon the sea in ships,
   that do business on the great waters,
24 These men see the works of Jehovah,
   and his wonders in the ocean-gulf.
25 For he spake, and caused a stormy wind to appear
   which lifted up the waves thereof;
26 They went up to the sky, they came down to the abysses,
   their soul melted away in the trouble;
27 They reeled and staggered like a drunken man,
   and all their wisdom was swallowed up.
28 But they cried unto Jehovah in their strait,
   and he brought them out of their distresses.
29 He turned the storm into a soft air,
   and their waves were hushed.
30 Then were they glad, because they were quieted,
   and he led them to their wished-for haven.
31 O let these give thanks to Jehovah for his kindness,
   and for his wondrous works to the children of men;
32 Let them exalt him also in the congregation of the people,
   and praise him in the company of the elders.

(Appendix.)

33 He turned rivers into a wilderness,
   and springs of water into thirsty ground;
34 A fruitful land into saltness
   for the wickedness of them that dwell therein.
35 He turned the wilderness into a standing water,
   and dry ground into springs of water;
36 And there he made the hungry to dwell,
   and they founded a city of habitation.

37 They sowed fields and planted vineyards,
  and obtained fruits of increase.
38 He blessed them, and they multiplied exceedingly,
  and he caused not their cattle to be minished.

39 And when they were minished and brought low
  through oppression of trouble and heaviness,
41 He set the needy secure from affliction,
  and made him families like a flock;
42 The upright see it, and rejoice,
  and all unrighteousness stops its mouth.

43 Whoso is wise, let him observe these things,
  and let them understand the kindnesses of Jehovah.

PSALM CVIII.
See Psalm LVII. 7-11, LX. 5-12.

CIX^e. O GOD of my praise, hold not thy peace,
  2 For the mouth of ungodliness and deceit have they opened upon me,
  they have spoken against me with lying tongue;
3 And with words of hatred have they surrounded me,
  and fought against me without a cause.
4 In return for love, they behave as mine adversaries,
  whilst I am all prayer;
5 Yea, they render me evil for good,
  and hatred for my love.

6 Set thou an ungodly man over him.
  and let an adversary stand at his right hand.

7 When he is accused, let him go forth condemned,
   and let his prayer become sin.
8 Let his days be few ;
   his store let another take.
9 Let his children be orphans,
   and his wife a widow.
10 Let his children be vagabonds, and beg,
   yea, let them be driven from their desolate homes.
11 Let the creditor ensnare all that he has,
   and let foreigners take his labour for a prey.
12 Let him have none that continues kindness to him,
   neither any that has pity on his orphans.
13 Let his posterity be cut off as their doom,
   in the next generation let their name be blotted out.
14 Let the iniquity of his fathers be mentioned before Jehovah,
   and the sin of his mother—let it not be blotted out.
15 Let them be over against Jehovah continually,
   and let him cut off their memory from the earth.

16 And that because he thought not to show loving-kindness,
   but persecuted the afflicted, needy man,
   yea, the heart-broken, that he might murder him,
17 And he loved cursing (so it will come to him),
   and delighted not in blessing (so it will be far from him) ;
18 And clothed himself with cursing even as with his robe,
   (so it will come into his inward parts like water,
   and like oil into his bones.)

19 Let it be unto him as a vesture wherein he wraps himself,
    and as a girdle wherewith he binds himself continually.
20 Be these the wages of mine adversaries from Jehovah,
    and of them that speak evil against my soul.

21 And thou, Jehovah Adonai, do nobly for me for thy name's sake;
    because thy lovingkindness is so good, deliver thou me.
22 For afflicted am I, and needy,
    and my heart is wounded within me:
23 Like a shadow when it stretches out, I disappear;
    I am shaken off as the locust:
24 My knees totter from fasting,
    and my flesh falls away into leanness:
25 And I—I am become a reproach unto them,
    when they see me they shake their head.

26 Help me, Jehovah my God,
    save me, according to thy lovingkindness:
27 That they may know that this is thy hand,
    and that thou, Jehovah, hast done it.
28 They may curse, but thou dost bless;
    when they arise, they will be confounded,
    but thy servant will rejoice.
29 Mine adversaries will be clothed with disgrace,
    and wrap themselves in their shame as in a mantle.
30 I will give great thanks unto Jehovah with my mouth,
    and praise him in the midst of many,
31 Because he stands at the right hand of the needy,
    to save him from those that judge his soul.

CX^e. THE oracle of Jehovah unto my Lord,
"Sit thou at my right hand,
until I make thine enemies
a footstool for thy feet."

2 The sceptre of thy strength shall Jehovah
stretch forth from Zion;
"Have thou sway in the midst of thine enemies."

3 Thy people are self-devoted in the day of thy warfare
upon the holy mountains;
from the womb, from the very dawn,
thy youth belong to thee.

4 Jehovah hath sworn, and he will not repent,
"Thou art a priest for ever
after the manner of Melchizedek."

5 The Lord is at thy right hand;
he will shatter kings in the day of his anger.
6 He will give doom among the nations;
he will fill with corpses; he will smite the heads
on a wide land.
7 Of the torrent shall he drink in the way;
therefore shall he lift up his head.

CXI. HALLELUJAH.
I will thank Jehovah with my whole heart,
in the council and assembly of the upright.

2 Great are the works of Jehovah,
  studied of all that delight therein.
3 Glorious and grand is his doing,
  and his righteousness abides for ever.
4 A memorial has he made for his wonders:
  Jehovah is full of pity and compassion.
5 Food has he given unto them that fear him,
  he will ever be mindful of his covenant.
6 The might of his works has he declared to his people,
  Giving them the heritage of the nations.
7 The works of his hands are truth and justice,
  all his behests are faithful;
8 They are established eternally and for ever,
  wrought out in truth and uprightness.
9 He sent deliverance unto his people,
  he has appointed his covenant for ever;
  holy and awful is his name.
10 The fear of Jehovah is the choicest of wisdom,
  good discernment have all such as practise them;
  his praise abides eternally.

CXII. HALLELUJAH.
  Happy the man that fears Jehovah,
  that delights much in his commandments.
2 Mighty on earth shall be his seed;
  the generation of the upright shall be blessed.
3 Wealth and riches are in his house,
  and his righteousness abides eternally.
4 Unto the upright there beams a light in the darkness,
  (unto him who is) pitiful, compassionate, and righteous.

5 It is well with the man that shows pity and lends;
     he will maintain his cause in the judgment.
6 For he shall never be moved;
     the righteous shall be had in everlasting remembrance.
7 He shall not be afraid of evil tidings;
     stedfast is his heart, trusting in Jehovah.
8 Established is his heart, he shall not be afraid,
     until he look his fill upon his enemies.
9 He has scattered abroad, he has given to the poor;
     his righteousness abides eternally:
     his horn shall be exalted in glory.
10 The ungodly shall see it and be vexed,
     he shall gnash with his teeth and melt away;
     the desire of the ungodly shall perish.

CXIII[e]. HALLELUJAH.

Praise, O ye servants of Jehovah,
praise the name of Jehovah.
2 Blessed be the name of Jehovah
     from henceforth even for ever.
3 From the rising of the sun unto the going down thereof
     the name of Jehovah is to be praised.

4 High is Jehovah above all nations,
     above the heavens is his glory.
5 Who is like unto Jehovah our God,
     that dwells so high,
     that looks so low—
     in heaven and on earth?

6 That raises the helpless out of the dust,
   and out of the dunghill lifts the needy,
7 To give him a home with princes,
   even with the princes of his people;
8 That gives the barren housewife a home
   as the joyful mother of her children.
       Hallelujah.

CXIV. WHEN Israel went forth from Egypt,
       The house of Jacob from a strange-speaking people,
2 Judah became his sanctuary,
   Israel his dominion.

3 The sea saw and fled,
   Jordan turned backward.
4 The mountains skipped like rams,
   the hills like the young of the flock.

5 What ails thee, O thou sea, that thou fleest?
   thou Jordan, that thou turnest back?
6 Ye mountains, that ye skip like rams?
   ye hills, like the young of the flock?

7 Be in pain, thou earth, at the presence of the Lord,
   at the presence of the God of Jacob;
8 Who turns the rock into a standing water,
   flint-stone into a fountain of water.

CXV. NOT unto us, Jehovah, not unto us,
       but unto thy name give glory,
   for thy lovingkindness and for thy truth's sake.

2 Wherefore should the heathen say,
    "Where, pray, is their God?"
3 Whereas our God is in heaven,
    whatsoever he pleases works he out.

4 (But) their idols are silver and gold,
    the handiwork of men;
5 Mouths have they, but they speak not,
    eyes have they, but they see not;
6 Ears have they, but they hear not,
    noses have they, but they smell not;
7 As for their hands, they handle not,
    as for their feet, they walk not;
    no sound give they with their throats.
8 They that made them shall become like unto them,
    even every one that trusts in them.

9 O Israel, trust thou in Jehovah,
    he is their help and their shield.
10 O house of Aaron, trust ye in Jehovah,
    he is their help and their shield.
11 Ye that fear Jehovah, put your trust in Jehovah,
    he is their help and their shield.
12 Jehovah has been mindful of us; he will bless—
    will bless the house of Israel,
    will bless the house of Aaron,
13 Will bless them that fear Jehovah,
    small as well as great.

14 Jehovah add to you,
    to you and to your children!
15 Blessed may ye be of Jehovah,
    who made heaven and earth!
16 The heavens are the heavens of Jehovah,
    but the earth has he given to the children of men.

17 The dead are not they that praise Jah,
   neither all such as have gone down into Silence.
18 But *we* will bless Jah,
   from henceforth even for ever.
      Hallelujah.

CXVI. I LOVE Jehovah, for he hears
         the voice of my supplications.
2 For he has inclined his ear unto me,
   and (therefore) I will call as long as I live.
3 The cords of Death had encompassed me,
   and the straits of Hades had come upon me;
   I found trouble and heaviness.
4 Then called I on the name of Jehovah,
   "Ah, Jehovah! deliver my soul."

5 Full of pity is Jehovah, and righteous,
   yea, our God is compassionate.
6 Jehovah preserves the simple,
   I was brought low, and he saved me.
7 Return unto thy rest, O my soul,
   for Jehovah has dealt bountifully with thee.
8 For thou hast rescued my soul from death,
   mine eye from tears,
   my foot from stumbling.
9 I shall walk before Jehovah
   in the lands of the living.

10 I believed when (thus) I spoke,
    though I was sore afflicted,
11 Though I had said in mine alarm,
    "All men are liars."

12 What can I render unto Jehovah
   for all his bounties unto me?
13 I will take the cup of salvations,
   and call upon the name of Jehovah.
14 My vows will I pay unto Jehovah,
   I would pay them before all his people.

15 A grave thing in the sight of Jehovah
   is the death of his loving ones.
16 Ah, (help me still,) Jehovah! for I am thy servant,
   I am thy servant, the son of thy handmaid;
   * * * thou hast loosed my bonds.
17 I will offer to thee the sacrifice of thanksgiving,
   and will call upon the name of Jehovah.
18 My vows will I pay unto Jehovah,
   I would pay them before all his people,
19 In the courts of the house of Jehovah,
   in the midst of thee, O Jerusalem.
       Hallelujah.

CXVII. O PRAISE Jehovah, all ye nations,
         laud him, all ye peoples.
2 For his lovingkindness is mighty over us,
   and the truth of Jehovah endures for ever.
       Hallelujah.

CXVIII. O THANK ye Jehovah, for he is good,
          for his lovingkindness endures for
   ever.

2 O let Israel say
   that his lovingkindness endures for ever.
3 O let the house of Aaron say
   that his lovingkindness endures for ever.
4 O let them that fear Jehovah say
   that his lovingkindness endures for ever.

5 From out of the straits I called upon Jah ;
   Jah answered me in a broad place.
6 Jehovah is on my side ; I will not fear ;
   what can man do unto me?
7 Jehovah is on my side, among my helpers,
   therefore shall I look my fill upon them that hate me.
8 It is better to take refuge in Jehovah
   than to put any confidence in man.
9 It is better to take refuge in Jehovah
   than to put any confidence in princes.

10 All nations have come about me,
   in Jehovah's name surely I will mow them down.
11 They have come about me, yea, they have come about me,
   in Jehovah's name surely I will mow them down.
12 They have come about me like bees,
   they are extinct like a fire of thorns,
   in Jehovah's name surely I will mow them down.

13 Thou hast thrust sore at me that I might fall,
   but Jehovah has helped me.
14 Jah is my strength and my song,
   therefore he became my salvation.
15 The sound of a ringing shout of salvation
   is in the tents of the righteous ;
   the right hand of Jehovah does valiantly.

16 The right hand of Jehovah is exalted;
    the right hand of Jehovah does valiantly.

17 I shall not die but live,
    and tell out the works of Jehovah.
18 Jehovah has chastened me indeed,
    but he has not given me over unto death.

19 "Open to me the gates of righteousness,
    that I may enter into them, and give thanks unto Jah."
20 "This is the gate of Jehovah,
    the righteous may enter into it."
21 I will give thanks unto thee, for thou didst answer me,
    and become my salvation.
22 The stone which the builders rejected
    is become the head stone of the corner.
23 This was by Jehovah's appointing,
    wondrous is it in our eyes.

24 This is the day which Jehovah has made,
    let us exult and rejoice in it.
25 Ah, Jehovah! grant us, I pray, salvation;
    Ah, Jehovah! grant us, I pray, prosperity.

26 Blessed be he that comes in the name of Jehovah,
    we bless you from the house of Jehovah.
27 Jehovah is the Strong, for he has given us light;
    bind the victim with cords
    even unto the horns of the altar.

28 Thou art my Strong One, and I will thank thee,
   my God, I will exalt thee.
29 O give thanks unto Jehovah, for he is good,
   for his lovingkindness endures for ever.

CXIX^e. ALEF.

1 HAPPY those that are blameless in their way, that walk in the law of Jehovah!
2 Happy those that keep his testimonies, that seek him with their whole heart,
3 That also have not worked iniquity, but walked in his ways!
4 Thou hast appointed thy behests to be observed exceedingly.
5 O that my ways were established, that I might observe thy statutes!
6 Then shall I not be ashamed, whilst I look unto all thy commandments.
7 I will thank thee with an unfeigned heart when I learn thy righteous ordinances.
8 Thy decrees will I observe; O forsake me not utterly!

BETH.

9 Wherewith shall a young man cleanse his path, to keep himself after thy word?
10 With my whole heart have I inquired after thee; let me not wander from thy commandments.
11 Thy saying have I treasured within my heart, that I should not sin against thee.
12 Blessed art thou, Jehovah; teach me thy decrees.

13 With my lips have I rehearsed all the ordinances of thy mouth.
14 In the way of thy testimonies I have as great a joy as in all manner of riches.
15 I will muse upon thy behests, and look towards thy paths.
16 I will solace myself with thy statutes; I will not forget thy word.

GIMEL.

17 Deal bountifully with thy servant that I may live; so will I heed thy word.
18 Uncover mine eyes that I may behold wondrous things out of thy law.
19 I am a sojourner upon earth; hide not thy commandments from me.
20 My soul is crushed with longing for thine ordinances at all times.
21 Thou hast rebuked the proud, the accursed ones, who wander from thy commandments.
22 Roll away from me reproach and contempt, for thy testimonies have I kept.
23 Yea, princes sit and speak against me; thy servant muses upon thy statutes.
24 Yea, thy testimonies are my solace, and my counsellors.

DALETH.

25 My soul cleaves unto the dust; revive me according to thy word.
26 I have rehearsed my ways, and thou hast answered me; teach me thy statutes.
27 Make me to understand the way of thy behests, so will I muse on thy wondrous works.

28 My soul drops tears for very heaviness; O raise me up according to thy word!
29 Remove from me the way of falseness, and grant me thy law graciously.
30 The way of faithfulness have I chosen; thine ordinances have I set (before me).
31 I cleave unto thy testimonies; Jehovah, make me not ashamed.
32 I will run the way of thy commandments, for thou dost enlarge my heart.

HE.

33 Point out to me, Jehovah, the way of thy statutes, and I will keep it to the last.
34 Give me understanding, and I will keep thy law; yea, I will observe it with my whole heart.
35 Direct me in the track of thy commandments, for therein do I delight.
36 Incline my heart unto thy testimonies, and not unto unjust gain.
37 Turn away mine eyes from beholding vanity; revive me in thy ways.
38 Ratify thy promise unto thy servant, which leads to thy fear.
39 Turn away my reproach which I dread, for thine ordinances are good.
40 Behold, I long after thy behests: revive me in thy righteousness.

VAU.

41 And let thy lovingkindnesses come unto me, Jehovah, even thy salvation, according unto thy promise.
42 And I shall have words to answer him that reproaches; for my trust is in thy word.

43 And snatch not the word of truth utterly out of my mouth, for I have waited on for thine ordinances.
44 So would I keep thy law continually for ever and ever,
45 And would walk at large, for I study thy behests,
46 And would speak of thy testimonies before kings, and not be ashamed.
47 Yea, I will solace myself with thy commandments which I love,
48 And will lift up my hands unto thy commandments which I love, and muse upon thy statutes.

ZAIN.

49 Remember (thy) word unto thy servant, seeing that thou hast caused me to hope.
50 This is my comfort in my affliction, that thy promise has quickened me.
51 The proud have had me greatly in derision; I have not declined from thy law.
52 I have remembered thine ordinances which are of old, Jehovah, and have received comfort.
53 A fever-glow has seized upon me because of the ungodly that forsake thy law.
54 Thy statutes have been to me for melodies in the house of my sojourning.
55 I have remembered thy name in the night, Jehovah, and have observed thy law.
56 This good has been mine, that I have kept thy behests.

KHETH.

57 My portion art thou, Jehovah; I have resolved to heed thy words.

58 I intreated thy favour with my whole heart; have pity upon me, according to thy promise.
59 I thought on my ways, and turned my feet unto thy testimonies.
60 I made haste and delayed not to keep thy commandments.
61 The cords of the ungodly have wound about me; I have not forgotten thy law.
62 At midnight I arise to give thanks unto thee because of thy righteous ordinances.
63 I am a companion of all them that fear thee and of those that observe thy behests.
64 Of thy lovingkindness, Jehovah, the earth is full; teach me thy statutes.

TETH.

65 Thou hast dealt graciously with thy servant, O Jehovah, according unto thy word.
66 Train me to rightness of judgment and perception, for I have believed thy commandments.
67 Before I was afflicted, I went astray, but now have I heeded thy sayings.
68 Thou art good, and doest good; teach me thy statutes.
69 The proud have forged a lie against me; I with my whole heart will keep thy behests.
70 Their heart is as gross as fat; I have solaced myself with thy law.
71 It is good for me that I was afflicted, that I might learn thy statutes.
72 The law of thy mouth is better unto me than thousands of gold and silver.

YOD.

73 Thy hands made me and fashioned me; give me understanding that I may learn thy commandments.

74 They that fear thee will be glad when they see me, for I have waited on for thy word.

75 I know, Jehovah, that thy judgments are righteous, and that thou in faithfulness hast afflicted me.

76 O let thy lovingkindness come forth to comfort me, according to thy promise unto thy servant.

77 Let thy compassions come unto me that I may live, for thy law is my solace.

78 The proud shall be ashamed, for they have lyingly distorted me; as for me, I will muse upon thy behests.

79 They that fear thee shall turn unto me, and they that know thy testimonies.

80 Let my heart be sound in thy statutes, that I be not ashamed.

CAF.

81 My soul pines for thy salvation; I have waited on for thy word.

82 Mine eyes pine for thy promise, saying, When wilt thou comfort me?

83 For I am become as a wine-skin in the smoke; thy testimonies do I not forget.

84 How many are the days of thy servant; when wilt thou execute judgment on them that persecute me?

85 The proud have digged pitfalls for me, they that are not after thy law.

86 All thy commandments are faithfulness; they persecute me lyingly; give me thy help.

87 They had almost made an end of me upon earth, but I forsook not thy behests.
88 Revive me after thy lovingkindness, so shall I observe the testimony of thy mouth.

LAMED.

89 Thy word, Jehovah, is fixed for ever in heaven.
90 Age upon age endureth thy faithfulness; thou didst settle the earth, and it stood.
91 They stand this day according to thine ordinances, for all creatures are thy servants.
92 Unless thy law had been my solace, I should then have perished in mine affliction.
93 I will never forget thy behests, for with them thou hast quickened me.
94 I am thine, O save me, for I have studied thy behests.
95 The ungodly have waited for me to destroy me; I will give close heed to thy testimonies.
96 To all perfection I have seen a limit; thy commandment is exceeding broad.

MEM.

97 O how I love thy law! it is my meditation all the day.
98 Thy commandments make me wiser than mine enemies, for they are mine for ever.
99 I am prudent above all my teachers, for thy testimonies are a meditation unto me.
100 I have more understanding than the aged, for I keep thy behests.
101 I have withheld my feet from every evil path, that I may heed thy word.

102 From thine ordinances have I not departed, for thou thyself hast instructed me.
103 How smooth are thy sayings unto my palate! yea, more than honey to my mouth.
104 Through thy behests I get understanding; therefore do I hate every false path.

NUN.

105 Thy word is a lamp unto my foot, and a light unto my track.
106 I have sworn, and have performed it, to observe thy righteous ordinances.
107 I am afflicted very sore; quicken me, Jehovah, according to thy word.
108 Accept, I beseech thee, Jehovah, the freewill offerings of my mouth, and teach me thine ordinances.
109 My soul is in my hand continually, but I do not forget thy law.
110 The ungodly have laid a snare for me, but I have not gone astray from thy behests.
111 Thy testimonies have I claimed as my heritage for ever, for they are the very joy of my heart.
112 I have inclined my heart to perform thy statutes, for ever, even to the last.

SAMECH.

113 I hate the double-minded, but thy law do I love.
114 Thou art my covert and my shield; I wait on for thy word.
115 Depart from me, ye evil-doers; I would keep the commandments of my God.
116 Sustain me, according to thy promise, that I may live, and let me not be ashamed of my hope.

117 Hold thou me up, and I shall be saved; so will I have regard unto thy statutes continually.
118 Thou makest light of all them that wander from thy statutes, for their self-deceit is but a lie.
119 All the ungodly of the earth I account as dross; therefore I love thy testimonies.
120 My flesh shudders for fear of thee, and I am afraid of thy judgments.

AIN.

121 I have practised justice and righteousness; thou wilt not leave me to mine oppressors.
122 Be surety for thy servant for good; let not the proud oppress me.
123 Mine eyes pine for thy salvation and for thy righteous promise.
124 Deal with thy servant according to thy loving-kindness, and teach me thy statutes.
125 I am thy servant, give me understanding, that I may know thy testimonies.
126 It is time for Jehovah to do valiantly; they have made void thy law.
127 Therefore do I love thy commandments above gold, yea, above fine gold.
128 Therefore have I chosen all thy behests; every false way have I hated.

PE.

129 Marvellous are thy testimonies, therefore has my soul kept them.
130 The opening of thy words gives light; it gives understanding to the simple.
131 I rent wide my mouth and panted, for I longed after thy commandments.

132 Turn towards me and have pity upon me, as is just unto those that love thy name.
133 Establish my steps by thy sayings, and let not aught of wickedness tyrannize over me.
134 Set me free from the oppression of man, so will I observe thy behests.
135 Make thy face to shine upon thy servant, and teach me thy statutes.
136 Mine eyes run down in rills of water, because men keep not thy law

SADE.

137 Righteous art thou, Jehovah, and straight are thine ordinances.
138 In righteousness hast thou appointed thy testimonies and in exceeding faithfulness.
139 My zeal hath even extinguished me, because my foes have forgotten thy words.
140 Thy promise is well tried in the fire, and thy servant loveth it.
141 I am small and of no reputation; thy behests do I not forget.
142 Thy righteousness is right for ever, and thy law is truth.
143 Distress and anguish have come upon me; thy commandments are my solace.
144 Thy testimonies are right for ever; give me understanding that I may live.

KOF.

145 I have called with my whole heart, answer me; thy statutes, Jehovah, would I keep.
146 I have called unto thee, save me; so will I observe thy testimonies.

147 Early in the twilight have I cried for help; I have waited on for thy word.
148 Mine eyes outgo the night-watches that I may muse upon thy sayings.
149 Hearken to my voice after thy lovingkindness; revive me, Jehovah, according to thine ordinances.
150 They draw near that pursue deeds of malice, that have gone far from thy law.
151 Thou, Jehovah, art near, and all thy commandments are truth.
152 Long since have I known from thy testimonies that thou hast grounded them for ever.

RESH.

153 Behold my affliction and rescue me, for I do not forget thy law.
154 Plead thou my cause and release me; revive me according to thy promise.
155 Far is salvation from the ungodly, for they inquire not after thy statutes.
156 Thy compassions are many, Jehovah; revive me according to thine ordinances.
157 Many are my persecutors and my foes; I have not declined from thy testimonies.
158 I beheld the unfaithful, and had loathing, because they heeded not thy sayings.
159 Behold how I love thy precepts; revive me, Jehovah, according to thy lovingkindness.
160 The sum of thy word is truth, and each of thy righteous ordinances is everlasting.

SHIN.

161 Princes have persecuted me without a cause, but my heart throbs fearfully at thy word.

162 I rejoice over thy sayings as one that finds great spoil.
163 I hate and abhor lying; thy law do I love.
164 Seven times a day do I praise thee because of thy righteous ordinances.
165 Great peace have they that love thy law, and for them there is no stumbling.
166 I have hoped for thy salvation, Jehovah, and thy commandments have I done,
167 My soul has heeded thy testimonies; yea, I have loved them exceedingly.
168 I have heeded thy behests and thy testimonies, for all my ways are before thee.

TAU.

169 Let my piercing cry come near before thee, Jehovah; give me understanding, according to thy word.
170 Let my supplication come before thee; deliver me, according to thy promise.
171 My lips shall gush forth with praise that thou teachest me thy statutes.
172 My tongue shall bear record of thy sayings, that all thy commandments are righteousness.
173 Let thine hand come forth to help me, for thy behests have I chosen.
174 I long, Jehovah, for thy salvation, and thy law is my solace.
175 Let my soul but live, and it shall praise thee, and let thine ordinances help me.
176 I wander like a lost sheep; seek thy servant, for I do not forget thy commandments.

CXX. UNTO Jehovah in my straitness
         I called, and he answered me.
2 Jehovah, deliver my soul from the lying lip,
    from the deceitful tongue.

3 What shall one give unto thee, and what more give
       unto thee,
    O deceitful tongue?
4 Arrows of a mighty man, sharpened ones,
    with glowing coals of broom.

5 Woe is me that I sojourn in Meshech,
    that I dwell beside the tents of Kedar!
6 Long enough has my soul had her dwelling
    beside one that hates peace.
7 I am all peace, but if I speak,
    they are bent on war.

CXXI. I WILL lift up mine eyes unto the moun-
          tains:
    whence will my help come?
2 My help comes from beside Jehovah,
    who made the heaven and the earth.

3 He cannot suffer thy foot to waver,
    he that keeps thee cannot slumber.
4 Behold, he that keeps Israel
    shall neither slumber nor sleep.

4 Jehovah is he that keeps thee,
   Jehovah is thy shade upon thy right hand.
5 The sun shall not smite thee by day,
   nor the moon by night.

6 Jehovah shall keep thee from all evil;
   he shall keep thy soul.
7 Jehovah shall keep thy going out and thy coming in
   from henceforth even for ever.

CXXII. I WAS glad when they said unto me,
   "Let us go to the house of Jehovah."

2 Our feet stand at last
   within thy gates, O Jerusalem.

3 Jerusalem, that art built up as a city
   that is well compact together,

4 Whither the tribes go up,
   even the tribes of Jah,

5 According to the ordinance for Israel,
   to give thanks unto the name of Jehovah.

6 For there are set thrones of judgment,
   even the thrones of the house of David.

7 Pray for the peace of Jerusalem:
   prosperous be they that love thee.

8 Peace be within thy rampart,
   prosperity within thy palaces.

9 For my brethren and companions' sakes
   I would wish thee peace.

10 For the sake of the house of Jehovah our God
   I would seek thy good.

CXXIII. UNTO thee have I lifted up mine eyes,
          O thou that art seated in the heavens!
2 Behold, as the eyes of servants
   are upon the hand of their masters,
   as the eyes of a handmaid
   are upon the hand of her mistress,
   so our eyes are upon Jehovah our God,
   until he have pity upon us.
3 Have pity upon us, Jehovah, have pity upon us,
   for we are but too full of contempt.
4 Our soul is but too full
   of the mocking of them that are at ease,
   the contempt of the haughty.

CXXIV. HAD not Jehovah himself been on our side,
   thus let Israel say,
2 Had not Jehovah himself been on our side,
   when men rose up against us,

3 Then would they have swallowed us up alive,
   when their anger was so hot against us.
4 Then would the waters have overwhelmed us,
   the torrent would have gone over our soul,

5 Then would they have gone over our soul—
    the raging waters.

6 Blessed be Jehovah, who gave us not up
    for a prey unto their teeth.
7 Our soul escaped as a bird
    out of the snare of the fowlers;
    the snare broke, and we
    made our escape.
8 Our help is in the name of Jehovah,
    who made heaven and earth.

CXXV. THEY that trust in Jehovah are like mount Zion,
    which cannot be shaken, but is seated for ever.
2 Jerusalem—mountains are round about her,
    Jehovah too is round about his people
    from henceforth even for ever.

3 For the sceptre of ungodliness shall not rest
    on the lot of the righteous,
    lest the righteous put forth
    their hands unto iniquity.

4 Do good, Jehovah, unto those that are good,
    and unto the upright in their hearts.
5 But those who make their paths to slant—
    Jehovah shall send them adrift with the workers of
        wickedness.
    Peace be upon Israel!

CXXVI. WHEN Jehovah brought back the captives of Zion,
we became like them that dream.
2 Then was our mouth filled with laughter,
and our tongue with ringing cries;
then said they among the nations,
Jehovah hath dealt nobly with them.
3 Jehovah dealt nobly indeed with us:
we became right glad.

4 Bring back our captives, Jehovah,
as the streams in the south land return.
5 They that sowed with tears
shall reap with ringing cries.
6 Weeping may a man go on his way
bearing seed for scattering;
with ringing cries shall he come home
bearing his sheaves.

CXXVII. EXCEPT Jehovah build the house,
they labour in vain thereat that build it:
except Jehovah keep watch over the city,
the watchman waketh but in vain.
2 It is in vain for you to rise up early,
and sit down late,
to eat the bread of painfulness;
surely he giveth his beloved sleep.

3 Behold, children are a heritage of Jehovah,
    the fruit of the womb is a reward.
4 As arrows in the hand of a mighty man,
    so are children of youth.
5 Happy is the man that has filled
    his quiver therewith;
    they shall not be ashamed when they speak
    with enemies in the gate.

CXXVIII. HAPPY is every one that fears Jehovah,
    that walks in his ways.
2 For thou shalt eat the labour of thy hands;
    happy art thou, and it is well with thee.

3 Thy wife shall be as a fruitful vine
    in the recesses of thy house;
    thy children like olive-plants
    round about thy table.

4 Behold, thus shalt the man be blessed
    that fears Jehovah.
5 Jehovah bless thee out of Zion!
    yea, do thou behold with glad eyes the good fortune of Jerusalem
    all the days of thy life;
6 Yea, do thou behold thy children's children.
    Peace be upon Israel!

CXXIX. MUCH indeed have they vexed me
from my youth up—
thus let Israel say—
2 Much indeed have they vexed me from my youth up,
yet they have not prevailed against me.

3 The ploughers ploughed upon my back,
and made their furrows long.
4 Jehovah is righteous, he hath cut asunder
the cord of the ungodly.
5 Let them turn back with shame
as many as hate Zion.

6 Let them be as the grass of the housetops
which withers before it be unsheathed;
7 With which the mower fills not his hand,
nor he that binds sheaves his bosom;
8 And they that go by say not,
"The blessing of Jehovah be upon you;
We bless you in the name of Jehovah."

CXXX. OUT of the depths have I cried unto
thee, Jehovah;
2 Lord, hearken to my voice;
attentive be thine ears
to the voice of my supplication.

3 If thou, Jah, shouldest bear iniquities in mind,
O Lord, who could stand?
4 Yea, but there is forgiveness with thee,
that thou mayest be feared.

5 I have waited for Jehovah, my soul hath waited,
   and in his word have I hoped.
6 My soul (waiteth) for the Lord,
   more than those that watch for the morning,
   than those that watch for the morning.

7 Let Israel hope in Jehovah,
   for with Jehovah there is lovingkindness,
   and with him is plenteous redemption;
8 And he shall redeem Israel
   from all his iniquities.

CXXXI. NOT haughty, Jehovah, is my heart,
   and not lofty are mine eyes;
neither have I been conversant with great matters,
or with things too high for me.
2 Surely I have composed and quieted my soul,
   as a weaned child in its mother's arms;
   my soul within me is like a weaned child.
3 Let Israel hope in Jehovah
   from henceforth even for ever.

CXXXII. JEHOVAH, remember unto David
   all his tribulation;
2 How he sware unto Jehovah,
   and vowed unto the Hero of Jacob,
3 "I will not go into the tent of my house,
   nor ascend the bed of my couch,
4 I will not give sleep to mine eyes,
   nor slumber to mine eyelids,

5 Until I find out a place for Jehovah,
    a habitation for the Hero of Jacob."

6 Behold, we heard of it at Ephrata,
    we found it in the fields of Jaar:
7 Let us go into his habitation,
    let us fall low before his footstool.
8 Arise, Jehovah, into thy resting-place,
    thou and the ark of thy strength.
9 Let thy priests be clothed with righteousness,
    and let thy loving ones ring out a glad cry.
10 For thy servant David's sake
    turn not away the face of thine anointed.

11 Jehovah has sworn unto David
    in truth—he will not go back from it:—
    " Of the fruit of thy body
    will I set upon thy throne;
12 If thy children keep my covenant,
    and mine ordinances that I shall teach them,
    their children also for ever
    shall sit upon thy throne."
13 For Jehovah has chosen Zion,
    he has desired it for his habitation.

14 " This is my resting-place for ever;
    here will I dwell, for I have desired it.
15 Her provision will I bless;
    her needy will I satisfy with bread.
16 Her priests also will I clothe with salvation,
    and her loving ones shall ring out a glad cry.
17 There will I make the horn of David to sprout,
    and set in order a lamp for mine anointed.
18 His enemies will I clothe with shame,
    but upon himself shall his crown shine."

CXXXIII. BEHOLD, how good and pleasant it is
for brethren to dwell together
kindly!
2 Like the fine oil upon the head
that runs down upon the beard, even Aaron's,
that runs down upon the opening of his garments.
3 Like the night-mist of Hermon that runs down
upon the mountains of Zion;
for there Jehovah commanded the blessing,
even life for evermore.

CXXXIV. BEHOLD, bless ye Jehovah,
all ye ervants of Jehovah,
who stand in Jehovah's house in the night-seasons.
2 Lift up your hands unto the sanctuary,
and bless Jehovah.
3 "Jehovah bless thee out of Zion,
he who made heaven and earth."

CXXXV. HALLELUJAH.
Praise ye the name of Jehovah;
praise him, O ye servants of Jehovah.
2 Ye that stand in the house of Jehovah,
in the courts of the house of our God.
3 Praise Jehovah, for Jehovah is good,
make melody unto his name, for it is pleasant.
4 For Jah hath chosen Jacob unto himself,
even Israel for his own possession.

5 For I am sure that Jehovah is great,
    and that our Lord is above all gods.
6 Whatsoever Jehovah pleases, that he works out
    in the heaven and in the earth,
    in the seas and in all abysses;
7 Who causes vapours to ascend from the end of the earth,
    who makes lightnings for the rain,
    who brings the wind out of his store-houses.

8 It is he who smote the first-born of Egypt,
    both of man and of beast;
9 Who sent tokens and prodigies
    into the midst of thee, O Egypt,
    upon Pharaoh and upon all his servants;
10 Who smote great nations,
    and slew mighty kings,
11 Sihon the king of the Amorites,
    and Og the king of Bashan,
    and all the kingdoms of Canaan,
12 And gave their land for an inheritance,
    an inheritance unto Israel his people.

13 Jehovah, thy name is everlasting,
    Jehovah, thy memorial endures unto all generations.
14 For Jehovah will right his people,
    and he will repent himself for his servants.
15 The idols of the heathen are silver and gold,
    the work of the hands of men.
16 Mouths have they, but they speak not,
    eyes have they, but they see not;
17 Ears have they, but they give no ear,
    neither is there any breath in their mouths.

18 They that made them shall become like unto them,
  even every one that trusts in them.

19 O house of Israel, bless ye Jehovah;
  O house of Aaron, bless ye Jehovah.
20 O house of Levi, bless ye Jehovah;
  ye that fear Jehovah, bless Jehovah.
21 Blessed be Jehovah out of Zion,
  that dwells at Jerusalem!
    Hallelujah.

CXXXVI[e]. Thank ye Jehovah, for he is good;
  for his kindness is everlasting.
2 Thank ye the God of gods; for his kindness is everlasting.
3 Thank ye the Lord of lords; for his kindness is everlasting.

4 To him that alone does great wonders; for his kindness is everlasting.
5 To him that by understanding made the heavens; for his kindness is everlasting.
6 To him that spread out the earth above the waters; for his kindness is everlasting.

7 To him that made great lights; for his kindness is everlasting.
8 The sun to rule by day; for his kindness is everlasting.
9 The moon and the stars to rule by night; for his kindness is everlasting.

10 To him that smote the Egyptians in their firstborn ; for his kindness is everlasting.
11 And brought out Israel from their midst ; for his kindness is everlasting.
12 With a strong hand and with a stretched-out-arm ; for his kindness is everlasting.

13 To him that cut the Red Sea into parts ; for his kindness is everlasting.
14 And made Israel to pass through the midst of it ; for his kindness is everlasting.
15 But shook off Pharaoh and his host into the Red Sea ; for his kindness is everlasting.

16 To him that led his people through the wilderness ; for his kindness is everlasting.
17 To him that smote great kings ; for his kindness is everlasting.
18 And slew glorious kings ; for his kindness is everlasting.

23 Who thought upon us in our abasement ; for his kindness is everlasting.
24 And rent us from our foes ; for his kindness is everlasting.
25 Who gives food to all flesh ; for his kindness is everlasting.

26 Give thanks unto the God of heaven ; for his kindness is everlasting.

CXXXVII^e. BY the rivers of Babylon—there we
  sat down and wept,
    when we remembered Zion:
2 Upon the poplars in their midst
    hanged we our lyres

3 For there they that led us captive asked of us
    words of song,
  And they that plundered us (required) joyousness,
    "Sing us one of the songs of Zion."

4 How can we sing Jehovah's songs
    in a foreign land?
5 If I forget thee, O Jerusalem,
    let the strength of my right hand dry up.

6 Let my tongue cleave to my palate,
    if I remember thee not,
    if I place not Jerusalem
    at the head of my joys.

7 Jehovah, remember unto the children of Edom
    the day of Jerusalem—
  Unto those who said, Rase it, rase it,
    even to the foundation thereof.

8 O daughter of Babylon, that art taken by storm,
    happy shall he be that pays thee back
    for what thou hast wrought on us.
9 Happy shall he be that takes and dashes
    thy children against the rocks.

CXXXVIII^e. I WILL thank thee with my whole heart;
  in the face of the gods will I make melody unto thee.
2 I will worship towards thy holy temple,
  and give thanks unto thy name,
  for thy lovingkindness and for thy truth;
  for thou hast magnified thy promise above all thy heavens.

3 In the day when I called thou answeredst me,
  and madest me bold with thy strength in my soul.
4 All the kings of the earth shall give thanks unto thee, Jehovah,
  when they shall have heard the words of thy mouth;

5 And shall sing of the ways of Jehovah,
  that great is the glory of Jehovah:
6 For Jehovah is high, and yet looks on the lowly,
  but the haughty he knows afar off.

7 If I walk in the midst of trouble, thou revivest me,
  thou stretchest forth thy hand against the wrath of mine enemies,
  and thy right hand saves me.
8 Jehovah will achieve all that concerns me;
  thy lovingkindness, Jehovah, is everlasting,
  the works of thine own hands abandon thou not!

CXXXIX^e. JEHOVAH, thou hast searched me out
and knowest me,
2 Thou knowest my downsitting and mine uprising,
thou understandest my thought afar off.
3 Whether I walk or lie down thou siftest me,
and art familiar with all my ways.
4 For before a word is on my tongue,
lo, thou, Jehovah, knowest it all.
5 Thou hast shut me in behind and before,
and laid thy hand upon me.
6 Too wonderful is (such) knowledge for me;
too lofty, I cannot attain to it.

7 Whither shall I go from thy spirit?
or whither shall I flee from thy face?
8 If I climb up into heaven, thou art there,
or if I make Hades my bed, lo, thou art there.
9 If I lift up the wings of the dawn,
and settle at the farther end of the sea,
10 Even there shall thy hand lead me,
and thy right hand take hold on me.
11 And if I say, "Let deep darkness screen me,
and the light about me be night,"
12 Even darkness is not dark with thee,
but the night is clear as the day—
the darkness is equal to the light.

13 For *thou* didst produce my reins,
and didst weave me together in my mother's womb.

14 I will thank thee, for I am fearfully and wonderfully
   made;
  marvellous are thy works,
  and my soul knows it right well.
15 My bones were not hid from thee,
  when I was made in secret,
  and curiously wrought in the underworld:
16 Mine unshapen mass thine eyes did see,
  and in thy book were they all written;
  (my) days were fashioned (already),
  when (as yet) there was none among them.
17 Unto me therefore O how weighty are thy thoughts,
   O God!
  O how vast are the sums of them!
18 If I reckon them, they are more in number than the
   sand;
  when I awake, I am still with thee.

19 O that thou wouldest slay the ungodly, O God!
  and that men of blood would depart from me!—
20 Who defy thee with outrageous acts,
  and pronounce thy name for falsehoods.
21 Do not I hate them, Jehovah, that hate thee?
  and have not I loathing at them that resist thee?
22 I hate them with a perfect hatred,
  I regard them as enemies.
23 Search me, O God, and know my heart,
  try me, and know my thoughts;
24 And see if there be any harmful way in me,
  and lead me in the way everlasting.

CXL*e*. RESCUE me, Jehovah, from the evil man,
from the man of violence guard thou me;
2 From those who plot evils in their heart,
and stir up wars continually,
3 Who have sharpened their tongue like a serpent—
adders' poison is under their lips.

4 Preserve me, Jehovah, from the hands of the ungodly,
from the man of violence guard thou me,
who purpose to trip up my feet.
5 The proud have hid snares for me and cords;
they have spread nets close by the track;
they have set gins for me.

6 I say unto Jehovah, Thou art my God;
give ear, Jehovah, to the voice of my supplications.
7 Jehovah Adonai, thou stronghold of my salvation,
thou hast screened my head in the day of armour.
8 Grant not, Jehovah, the desires of the ungodly,
let not his wicked plan succeed.

9 Let [not] them that encompass me lift up their head,
let the mischief of their own lips cover them;
10 Let them totter [from their place];
Jehovah rain hot coals upon them!
let him cause them to fall into the fire,
into nets that they rise not again

11 A slanderer shall have no continuance in the earth;
the violent man—evil shall hunt him with thrust
upon thrust.

12 Sure I am that Jehovah will maintain
   the cause of the afflicted—the right of the needy.
13 Truly the righteous shall give thanks unto thy name,
   and the upright shall dwell in thy presence.

CXLI^e.   JEHOVAH, I call upon thee, speed thee unto me;
   give ear unto my voice when I cry unto thee.
2 Let my prayer continue as incense before thee,
   the lifting up of my hands as the evening sacrifice.

3 Set a watch, Jehovah, before my mouth,
   guard the door of my lips.
4 Incline not my heart to any evil thing,
   to practise foul deeds wickedly
   with men that work naughtiness,
   and let me not eat of their dainties.

5 Let the righteous smite me in lovingkindness and
      correct me,
   it is oil for the head, which my head may not
      refuse;
      *   *   *   *
6 *   *   *   *   *
      *   *   *   *
7 As when one cleaves and breaks up the earth,
   our bones are scattered at the mouth of Hades.

8 For mine eyes are toward thee, Jehovah Adonai;
   in thee have I taken refuge, pour not out my soul.

9 Preserve me from the grasp of the snare which they
  have laid for me,
 and from the gins of them that work naughtiness.
10 The ungodly shall fall into their own nets together;
 [unhurt] shall *I* be, until I pass by.

CXLII.ᵉ With my voice do I cry unto Jehovah;
  with my voice unto Jehovah do I
  make my supplication:
2 I pour out my complaint before him,
 I display before him my trouble.

3 When my spirit faints within me,
  thou—thou knowest my path:
4 In the way wherein I walk
  they have hidden snares for me.

5 I look on the right and behold [on the left],
  but there is none that knows me again;
  no place is left to flee unto,
  there is none that cares for my soul.

6 I cry unto thee, Jehovah,
  I say, Thou art my refuge,
  my portion in the land of the living.

7 Attend unto my piercing cry,
  for I am become very weak;
  deliver me from them that pursue me,
  for they are too strong for me.

8 Bring forth my soul from prison,
    that I may give thanks unto thy name;
    the righteous shall glory in me,
    because thou dealest bountifully with me.

CXLIII. HEAR my prayer, Jehovah, give ear to my supplications;
    in thy faithfulness answer me in thy righteousness:
2 And enter not into judgment with thy servant,
    for none that lives can be righteous before thee.
3 For the enemy hath pursued my soul, crushed to the ground my life,
    made me to dwell in dark places, as those that have been long dead.
4 Therefore my spirit faints within me,
    my heart in the midst of me is bewildered.

5 I remember the days of old,
    I meditate upon all thy doing,
    I muse upon the work of thy hands.
6 I spread forth my hands unto thee,
    My soul is toward thee as a thirsty land.
7 Answer me, Jehovah, speedily,
    my spirit fails;
    hide not thy face from me,
    then should I be like unto them that have gone down into the pit.
8 Make me to hear thy lovingkindness in the morning,
    for in thee do I trust,
    make me to know the way wherein I should walk,
    for I lift up my soul unto thee.

9 Deliver me, Jehovah, from mine enemies;
   I have fled unto thee for refuge.

10 Teach me to do thy will, for thou art my God;
   let thy good spirit lead me in a level path.
11 For thy name's sake, Jehovah, revive me;
   in thy righteousness, O bring my soul out of trouble;
12 And in thy lovingkindness cut off mine enemies,
   and destroy all them that vex my soul;
   for I am thy servant.

CXLIV^e. BLESSED be Jehovah my Rock,
   who teaches my hands to war,
   my fingers to fight.
2 My castle and my fortress, my high tower, and my deliverer,
   my shield, and he in whom I take refuge,
   who subdues peoples under me.
3 Jehovah, what is the earth-born that thou takest notice of him?
   or the son of mortal man that thou so accountest of him?
4 Earth-born man is like unto a breath,
   his days are as a passing shadow.

5 Bow thy heavens, Jehovah, and come down,
   touch the mountains, so that they smoke.
6 Flash forth lightnings, and scatter them;
   shoot out thine arrows and confound them;

7 Stretch out thy hand from high heaven,
   rend me away and rescue me out of great waters,
   out of the hand of aliens,
8 Whose mouth speaks falsehood,
   and their right hand is a right hand of lies.

9 I would sing a new song unto thee, O God;
   with a ten-stringed harp would I make melody
      unto thee,
10 Who givest deliverance unto kings,
   and rescuedst David thy servant from the hurtful
      sword.

(Quotation from a lost Psalm.)

12 Because "our sons are as plants reared up tall in
      their youth,
   our daughters are as cornices carved in palace-
      fashion;
13 Our garners are full, affording all manner of store,
   our flocks increasing by thousands, yea, tens of
      thousands in our streets;
14 Our kine are great with young, * * *
   no breach, nor exile-train, nor woful cry in our
      broad places.
15 Happy the people that is in such a case;
   happy the people which has Jehovah for its God."

CXLV^e. I WILL extol thee, my God, O King,
            and bless thy name for ever and ever.
2 Every day will I bless thee,
   and praise thy name for ever and ever.

3 Great is Jehovah, and highly to be praised,
   and his greatness is unsearchable.
4 Let one generation celebrate thy works unto another,
   and let them declare thy mighty acts.
5 The excellent glory of thy grandeur shall be their theme,
   of thy wondrous deeds shall be my discourse.
6 Yea, they shall speak of the might of thy terrible acts,
   and I will tell out thy greatness.
7 The fame of thine abundant goodness shall they send as from a wellspring,
   and shall ring out thy righteousness.

8 Jehovah is full of pity and compassion,
   long-suffering and of great lovingkindness.
9 Jehovah is good unto all,
   and his compassion is over all his works.
10 All thy works shall give thanks unto thee, Jehovah,
   and thy loving ones shall bless thee.
11 They shall speak of the glory of thy kingdom,
   and shall talk of thy might,
12 To make known to the sons of men his mighty acts,
   and the excellent glory of his kingdom.
13 Thy kingdom is a kingdom of all æons,
   and thy dominion endures throughout all generations.
14 Jehovah upholds all them that fall,
   and lifts up all that are bowed down.

15 The eyes of all wait upon thee,
   and thou givest them their food in due season.
16 Thou openest thine hand,
   and satisfiest the desire of every living thing.

17 Righteous is Jehovah in all his ways,
and loving in all his works.
18 Jehovah is nigh unto all them that call upon him,
unto all that call upon him in truth.
19 He will fulfil the desire of them that fear him,
he will also hear their cry, and will save them.
20 Jehovah preserves all them that love him,
but all the wicked will he exterminate.
21 My mouth shall speak the praise of Jehovah,
and let all flesh bless his holy name for ever and
ever.
Hallelujah.

CXLVI. PRAISE Jehovah, O my soul.
2 I will praise Jehovah, as long as I
live ;
I will make melody unto Jehovah while I have
my being.
3 Put not your trust in nobles,
in the son of the earthborn who cannot save ;
4 When his breath goes forth he returns to his earth,
in the same day his thoughts perish.

5 Happy is he that hath the God of Jacob for his
help,
whose hope is in Jehovah his God ;
6 Who made heaven and earth,
the sea, and all that therein is,
who keeps truth for ever.
7 Who executes judgment for the oppressed,
who gives bread to the hungry.

8 Jehovah looses them that are bound,
  Jehovah opens the eyes of the blind,
  Jehovah lifts up them that are bowed down,
  Jehovah loves the righteous.
9 Jehovah preserves the strangers,
  he helps up the orphan and the widow,
  but the way of the ungodly he makes to slant.
10 Jehovah shall be king for ever,
  even thy God, O Zion, unto all generations.
    Hallelujah.

CXLVII^e. O PRAISE Jah, for it is good to make melody unto him,
  praise is seemly for our God.
2 Jehovah is the builder up of Jerusalem,
  he gathers together the outcasts of Israel.
3 It is he that heals the broken in heart,
  and binds up their painful wounds:
4 He reckons a number for the stars,
  and calls them all by names.
5 Great is our Lord, and rich in power,
  of his understanding there is no number.
6 Jehovah helps up the afflicted,
  but abases the ungodly to the ground.

7 Sing ye unto Jehovah with thanksgiving,
  make melody unto our God upon the lyre;
8 Who covers the heaven with clouds,
  who prepares rain for the earth,
  who makes the mountains to sprout with grass;
9 Who gives to the beast his food,
  to the young ravens which cry.

10 His pleasure is not in the strength of a horse,
   his delight is not in the legs of a man;
11 Jehovah delights in them that fear him,
   in them that wait for his lovingkindness.

12 Laud Jehovah, O Jerusalem,
   praise thy God, O Zion:
13 For he has strengthened the bars of thy gates,
   and has blessed thy children within thee.
14 It is he that has set thy borders in peace,
   that satisfies thee with the fat of wheat,
15 That sends his commandment to the earth—
   his word runs very swiftly,
16 That gives snow like wool,
   that scatters hoar-frost like ashes;
17 He casts forth his ice like pieces (of bread),
   who can stand before his cold?
18 He sends his word, and melts them;
   let him blow with his wind, and the waters will flow.
19 He declared his word unto Jacob,
   his statutes and ordinances unto Israel;
20 He has not done so to any nation,
   and as for his ordinances—men know them not.
       Hallelujah.

CXLVIIIc. HALLELUJAH.
   O praise Jehovah from the heavens,
   praise him in the heights.
2 Praise him all ye angels of his,
   praise him, all his host.

3 Praise him, sun and moon;
   praise him, all ye stars of light.

4 Praise him, ye heavens of heavens,
   and ye waters that are above the heavens.
5 Let them praise the name of Jehovah,
   for he commanded and they were created;
6 And he gave them a station for ever and ever,
   he made a decree which they may not transgress.

7 Praise Jehovah from the earth,
   ye dragons and all ye ocean-abysses;
8 Fire and hail, snow and smoke,
   Stormy wind fulfilling his word;
9 Mountains and all hills,
   fruit-trees and all cedars;

10 Wild beasts and all cattle,
   creeping things and winged birds;
11 Kings of the earth and all peoples,
   princes and all judges of the earth;
12 Youths in their prime and damsels too,
   aged men by the side of boys;

13 Let them praise the name of Jehovah,
   for his name alone is exalted,
   his grandeur above earth and heaven:
14 He has also exalted the horn of his people;
   [comely] is praise for all his loving ones,
   for the children of Israel, the people near unto him.
           Hallelujah.

CXLIX. HALLELUJAH.
Sing unto Jehovah a new song,
and his praise in the congregation of the loving.
2 Let Israel rejoice in him that made him,
let the children of Zion exult in their king.
3 Let them praise his name with dancing,
let them make melody unto him with the timbrel
and lyre.

4 For Jehovah delights in his people,
he adorns the afflicted with salvation.
5 Let the lovers of God triumph in glory,
let them sing aloud upon their beds.
6 Let lofty hymns divine be in their throat,
and a two-edged sword in their hand ;

7 To execute vengeance upon the nations,
punishments upon the peoples,
8 To bind their kings with chains,
and their most honourable with fetters of iron ;
9 To execute upon them the doom that is written—
an honour this to all his loving ones.
Hallelujah.

CL. HALLELUJAH.
Praise God in his sanctuary,
praise him in the firmament of his power ;
2 Praise him for his mighty acts,
praise him according to his manifold greatness ;

3 Praise him with the peal of the cornet,
    praise him with the harp and lyre ;
4 Praise him with the timbrel and dance,
    praise him with strings and pipe ;
5 Praise him with clanging cymbals,
    praise him with deep-sounding trumpets ;
6 Let everything that has breath praise Jah.
      Hallelujah.

EXPLANATIONS.

PSALM I. Prefaces are written last, and this prefatory psalm was evidently written during the fresh enthusiasm for Ezra's law-book (Ezra viii.). The author is a Pharisee of the better sort, to whom the law was a "law of liberty." He has taken to heart the parting words of the last prophet (Mal. iv. 4). Ps. xix. 8-14, is written in the same spirit.

Ver. 1. How delicately the psalmist distinguishes between the three degrees or forms of evil habits!

Ver. 3. *by water-courses.* By canals made for irrigation.

Ver. 5. *in the judgment.* When Jehovah sifts the Jewish community, and expels those who are not "Israelites indeed."

Ver. 6. *perishes.* Loses itself; fails to reach man's true end (*comp.* xxv. 8).

PSALM II. A lyric echo of the promises to David's seed in 2 Sam. vii. 12, 14-16, to be read with Ps. lxxxix. The psalmist "sees not yet" a Davidic empire worthy of "Jehovah's son," but trusts the Divine promise (see on ver. 8). What political event suggested the psalm, is uncertain.

Ver. 6. What impiety, *when I have established my king!*

Ver. 7. *my son.* So 2 Sam. vii. 14. Ps. lxxxix. 26. *this day.* The day that the king was anointed. *begotten.* Figuratively, in the sense of adoption.

Ver. 8. This promise does not occur in 2 Sam. vii., but may be compared with Ps. lxxxix. 27.

Ver. 12. *Kiss the Son.* "Kiss" as a token of friendly relations (2 Sam. x. 1). The word for "son" is a rare one (see Prov. xxxi. 2) adopted from the Chaldee. Some have thought the phrase corrupt or an interpolation; but at any rate we find another Chaldaism in ver. 9.

PSALM III. The morning prayer of a pious Israelite at a time of national danger from without.

Ver. 2 gives us the language either of open enemies or of desponding friends. *salvation.* Here in the sense of deliverance, but found also in that of welfare (l. 23, xci. 16, cxxxii. 16).

Ver. 4. The psalmist's constant experience that prayer is answered.

PSALM IV. An evening prayer, at a time of danger from within. The psalmist seeks to win over his enemies by expostulation.

Ver. 1. *have pity.* Not "have mercy." The idea is not that of sparing the guilty, but of being favourable.

Ver. 2. *vanity*, i.e. baseless accusations.

Ver. 3. *But see...* Recognize the contrast in the Divine treatment of me. I have been in danger as great before, and have been delivered.

Ver. 4. *Tremble.* Be shaken out of your proud security by the sight of the favour which I enjoy.

Ver. 5. True piety is both inward and outward. Inwardly, it is *trust*; outwardly, it is expressed in *the right sacrifices*, those which symbolize the devotion of the heart, as opposed to "false (or, hypocritical) offerings" (Isa. i. 13). *Comp.* li. 19, Deut. xxxiii. 19.

Ver. 7. The prayer of faith has been answered inwardly. The psalmist's spiritual joy is more intense than the husbandman's physical excitement at the feasts of ingathering.

Ver. 8. *at once.* No tossing before slumber comes. *alone*, either as an element of safety, or as a drawback which is only apparent (*comp.* John xvi. 32).

PSALM V. Another morning prayer.

Ver. 1. *my murmuring*, which none but God can interpret.

Ver. 3. (*my sacrifice*). "Spiritual sacrifices" (1 Pet. ii. 5).

Ver. 5. *naughtiness.* That which is morally worthless.

Ver. 7. How different is my own fate! *I ... can enter* (am allowed to enter) *thy house*—the grand pleasure of the psalmists.

Ver. 8. *thy way*, i.e. that which thou wouldst have me walk in. *level*, i.e. free from difficulties, moral or physical.

PSALM VI. Ver. 1. *not in thine anger*, "but with mildness and with perfect love," as the supposed Dante paraphrases.

Ver. 2. *my bones*. The bones often appear as the representatives of the whole body, and even of the whole nature of man. See *e.g.* xxxi. 10, xxxii. 3, xxxv. 10, li. 8.

Ver. 5. *in Death*. Another name for Hades. *See* Rev. i. 18, vi. 8, xx. 13, 14. *in Hades*. The Greek word for the underworld, the land of the Refaim or shades, is more familiar to English readers than the Hebrew Sheól, and the anachronism in using it is far less than that in using the Teutonic hell.

PSALM VII. Prayers and meditations of Israel personified.

Ver. 5. *my glory*, i.e. my soul (as xvi. 9, xxx. 12, lvii. 8). *a sentence* (in my favour) *thou hast commanded*; the language of faith which anticipates the answer to prayer.

Ver. 7. *the assemblage of the peoples*, viz., of the nations of the world, whom Jehovah is about to judge, including Israel (precisely as Isa. iii. 13, 14). *return thou over it*. It is implied that the sentences, for good or for evil, have already been pronounced.

Ver. 8. *my innocence*. It is the nation, not an individual, which asserts its innocence from the point of view of general obedience to the law (*comp.* Ps. xliv. 17-21). Humility had already become a virtue of individuals, but did not as yet characterize the nation.

Ver. 9. *the hearts and reins*, both regarded as the seats of the thoughts and feelings.

Ver. 12. *If any will not turn*. The psalmist passes abruptly to the general subject of the retribution in store for the transgressor. The continuation may, however, be by another writer.

Ver. 13. *aflame*. The "fiery darts" of Eph. vi. 16.

PSALM VIII. "A lyric echo of the history of creation." How small and yet how great is man!

Ver. 2. Paradoxical but true. The simplicity of children is a match for the cunning and the violence of the enemy, because these children trust in and praise Jehovah.

Ver. 3. Why is not the sun mentioned? Because the moon and the starry hosts give a deeper notion of infinity.

Ver. 5. *thou madest him*... The first or ideal man being modelled after God (Gen. i. 27).

PSALM IX. This and the next psalm originally formed but one, but such changes have been introduced, that it is better to retain the division into two parts. The original psalm was alphabetic, *i.e.* it consisted of 22 verses, beginning with the letters of the alphabet in succession.

Ver. 3, 4. The psalmist writes amidst the tokens of defeat which are also the tokens of God's judicial session.

Ver. 8. *give doom.* So Hereford and Purvey, "He gyueth doom to pore men" (Job. xxxvi. 6).

Ver. 6. *ruins.* The nations are identified with their lands.

Ver. 12. *he who requires blood*, i.e., God, who like the nearest kinsman demands blood for blood. *the afflicted.* A common phrase for the pious kernel of the Jewish people, often with the secondary meaning of "humble."

Ver. 13 14. The prayer which has now been answered. *gates of Death* (i.e. of Hades, *see* on vi. 5). So Ps. cvii. 18, Isa. xxxviii. 10. The Assyrian Hades had seven walls and gates; *comp.* Matt. xvi. 18.

PSALM X. Ver. 2. *they are caught.* The afflicted are probably meant, as the whole context describes the doings of the wicked.

Ver. 4. *The wicked.* . . . We should expect a verb to follow, such as "thinks." But the construction is suddenly changed.

Ver. 5. *His ways are stable*, i.e., he has no vicissitudes of fortune. *thy judgments.* . . . God's threatened judgments are to him as purely imaginary as God and as heaven. His eye cannot detect them.

Ver. 6. *bow down.* Like a statue hurled from its pedestal. *under his tongue*, in readiness for uttering, as lxvi. 17, cxl. 3.

Ver. 8. *the villages*, where bandits can least easily be resisted. *his eyes.* . . . "Like those of a tiger in the dark." *his strong ones.* Poetically for "his claws."

Ver. 15. *till thou find none.* Till the last atom of wickedness be removed.

Ver. 16. The psalmist's warrant for his prayer: a king, by the very conception of kingship, must execute judgment. Then the anticipated answer. "Prayer is possession" (E. Irving).

PSALM XI. Faith gives tranquillity in times of revolution.

Ver. 3. *the foundations*, viz., of the state regarded as a house. As lxxxii. 5.

Ver. 6. Lightning, thunderbolts, and simoom.

Ver. 7. *shall behold his countenance*. A promise of spiritual communion with God. In this life or the next? The psalmist is not in a mood to answer. He is close upon St. John's conception of "eternal life" as a present possession (*comp.* on xvii. 15).

PSALM XII. Ver. 1. *the man of love*. There is no English word to express the full meaning of the Hebrew. The "godly" and "saint" of King James's Bible fail to give the emotional tinge of Hebrew piety. Jehovah requires that a man should do his duty both to God and to his brother man with a certain warmth of feeling. Love and duty there are both implied: "love is *dutiful* in thought and deed." *the faithful*, i.e. the trustworthy.

Ver. 4. *With our tongue*. . . . The tongue is more than their faithful servant; it unweariedly suggests the most artful lies, the most terrifying threats, which are a stronghold to these wicked ones, as the praises of children are to Jehovah (viii. 2).

Ver. 6. *pure words*, with no admixture of falsehood. Purer than the purity of refined silver (*comp.* xviii. 30).

Ver. 8 is placed before ver. 7, because "this generation" points back to "the ungodly." A similar correction, xxxiv. 16, 17.

PSALM XIV. Compare another version in Ps. liii., where the name Jehovah is avoided.

Ver. 3. *It has all*, i.e. the entire human race.

Ver. 4. The search for piety has failed; the judgment will begin, and begin (as in Isa. iii. 13-15) with the great men of Israel. For the figure of eating, *comp.* Mic. iii. 3.

Ver. 7. Probably added when the psalm was adopted for liturgical use. Israel was then under a cloud, and longed for deliverance to come from Jehovah's throne.

PSALM XV. Against those who thought a merely formal worship enough (*comp* xxiv. 1-6, Isa. xxxiii. 14-16).

Ver. 1. *pavilion* (tent) is a synonym for house (xxvii. 5, lxi. 4).

Ver. 4. *He that gives not*. . . To the poor Israelite such a man lends gratuitously (xxxvii. 26, cxii. 5).

PSALM XVI. Ver. 3. The psalmist's friends are those of Jehovah. To he less exclusive, would injure his sense of communion with God, and his confidence in the divine protection. Possibly the *noble ones* are the priests ("hallowed princes," 1 Chr. xxiv. 5). Are we in Maccabean times? *Noble ones* implies a position of authority (Jer. xxv. 34-36).

Ver. 9. *my flesh*, i.e. my body.

Ver. 10. The psalmist is confident that his work in this world is not finished.

Ver. 11. *the path of life*, that on which life is to be found. A thought like St. John's.

PSALM XVII. The complaint of Israel personified, or of a pious Israelite, whose troubles are not personal, but those of his country; *comp.* ver. 11. The assertions of innocence are to be explained as in vii. 8.

Ver. 3, 4. The divine searcher will find me free from sin in thought, in word, and in deed; that is, sincerely faithful to the Law. *the robber*, taken as the type of lawlessness. Israel then was treated as an outlaw with no rights or claims for pity.

Ver. 10. *Their caul*, i.e. the membrane surrounding the heart (Hos. xiii. 8, A. V.).

Ver. 14. *in life*, i.e. in material life, as opposed to what St. John calls "eternal life." *See* on lxiii. 3. *whose belly*. The belly being regarded as the seat of greed and avarice; *comp.* Job xx. 21, "nothing escaped his eating."

Ver. 15. *As for me.* . . . . All need some happiness, and God lovingly supplies the need. "Thou in thy lifetime receivedst thy good things." But "as for me"—the poor, the persecuted —what is my portion? It is to "see thy face in righteousness" (*i.e.* in accordance with thy promise, Isa. xlii. 6, xlv. 13)—mystic communion with God, began in this life, and to be perfected "when I awake." *thine image.* But the letter of the psalm is bolder—"thy form."

PSALM XVIII. A thanksgiving-ode for the nation or for the Davidic family.

Ver. 4, 5. Death and Hades (*i.e.* the prince of Hades) are represented as hunters with cords and snares (*comp.* xlix. 15). *perdition.* The extreme degree of evil is meant, which is absolutely without a "soul of goodness." Perdition being parallel to Death and Hades, we are on the road to the personification of it as a demon (Belial); *see* 2 Cor. vi. 15.

Ver. 15. The effect of the earthquake (ver. 7) on the seas is mentioned out of its place, to smooth the transition to the figurative "many waters."

Ver. 25. *With the loving.* . . God meets man in the same spirit in which man meets God; *comp.* 1 Sam. ii. 30. The statement implies the idea of the covenant. God's lovingkindness and truth, another psalmist says, are for such as keep his covenant (xxv. 10). "Loving" was explained on xii. 1.

Ver. 31. *a rock.* An old synonym for God, more poetical than El (the strong one); *comp.* Deut. xxxii. (six times), Isa. xvii. 10, xxx. 29, xliv. 8.

Ver. 32. *my way*, i.e. my career. *Flawless*, i.e. unspoiled by sins or blunders.

Ver. 33. *upon my high places.* Upon the high places which I claim as mine by right, and which are the bulwark of my power. *Comp.* Deut. xxxii. 13, Isa. lviii. 14.

Ver. 35. *thy humility.* For the sense, *see* Isa. lvii. 18.

Ver. 43. *strifes of the people.* Such as are implied in verse 48 —civil wars.

PSALM XIX. Verses 1-6 probably formed part of a longer poem, as neither verse 6 nor verses 7-14 form a suitable close. It is only by an afterthought that the two parts of the psalm have been brought into relation, the sun being regarded as a type of the law of Jehovah. (*Comp.* Kant's two glorious things, the starry heavens and the conscience.) The latter part of the psalm is written in the spirit of Psalms i. and cxix.

Ver. 2. *Day unto day* . . . i.e. every day the heavens renew their testimony to God's glory.

Ver. 4. *Their voice*, either that of the heavens or of day and night. *in them*, i.e. in the heavens.

Ver. 12. *Lapses*, i.e. errors due to ignorance or inattention, opposed (as in the Levitical Law) to "presumptuous sins."

PSALM XX. Addressed to a king going forth to battle.

Ver. 3. *find* . . *fat*, i.e. accept. *Comp.* Gen. viii. 21, "and Jehovah smelled a sweet savour."

Ver. 5. *at thy salvation*, when it has been granted (*comp.*

xxi. 5). "Salvation" here, as often, = victory, regarded as God's gift.

Ver. 6. *Now am I sure.* . . A sacrifice has probably just been offered to make the war a "holy war" (*comp.* 1 Sam. xiii. 9). Strengthened faith is the result.

PSALM XXI. The people's joy at the victorious return of the king, who is addressed in verses 8-11. *Compare* a somewhat similar Assyrian Prayer for the King (*Records of the Past*, iii. 133-4, or better Schrader, *Istar* 72-5).

Ver. 6. *most blessed.* Literally, blessings, *i.e.* as in Bishop Heber's hymn, "all-blessing and all-blessed." *in thy presence.* The king being regarded as seated at Jehovah's right hand, where is "fulness of joys" (xvi. 11).

Ver. 9. *Thou shalt make them.* . . . *when thou appearest.* (Literally, at the time of thy face.) The actions of the king are identified with those of the heavenly king (*see* next line); hence a phrase is used which everywhere else refers to Jehovah. So lxxx. 16. "they shall perish at the rebuke of thy face."

PSALM XXII. An appeal for help from the depths of affliction, followed by a joyous announcement of the answer vouchsafed, and prophecies of its far-reaching effects, in which all nations, and even the departed, shall share. Who is the speaker? An imagined person, like Plato's wise man who at last is crucified? or the people of Israel personified? In order to answer this question, compare descriptions of the sufferings of Job, and of the servant of Jehovah (in the second part of Isaiah); also Psalms xxxv., lxix., and in general the parallel passages referred to below, which are only some out of a multitude.

Ver. 3. *the holy one*, devoted therefore to Israel, as Israel is to thee, and bound by covenant-promises to deliver thine inheritance. *who inhabitest.* . . . The "praises of Israel" are like the wings of the cherubim on which Jehovah is (or was) enthroned (*comp.* lxxx. 1, xcix. 1).

Ver. 6. *a worm and no man.* Comp. xli. 14, lii. 14, liii. 2. *despised of people.* Comp. Isa. xlix. 7.

Ver. 7. *they shake the head.* So xxxi. 11, xliv. 14, cix. 25, Lam. ii. 15.

Ver. 8. *has rolled it* . . . , i.e. has committed his cause entirely to Jehovah, careless of any other help. *Comp.* xxxvii. 5. *since he delights . . .*, viz. Jehovah.

Ver. 9. *out of the womb.* Of course an individual may be the speaker, but so also may the people personified (*comp.* Isa. xlviii. 8). *See* on Ps. lxxi.

Ver. 12. *strong ones of Bashan.* The "strong ones" are bulls, for which the pastures across Jordan were famous. *Comp.* for this symbolic phrase, Ezek. xxxix. 18, Am. iv. 1.

Ver. 15. *the dust of Death.* The Babylonian Hades is described as "the place where much dust is their nourishment" (Descent of Istar, l. 8). *Comp.* ver. 29 and xxx. 9.

Ver. 16. *they have dug . . .*, i.e. they bite pieces out of my hands and my feet, when I try to beat them off, and to escape. This feature in the description would have seemed more in place after ver. 17. The dogs torture the sufferer first with their insolent gaze, and then, when he seeks to escape from this, with their fangs.

Ver. 20. *my darling* (lit. my only one), *i.e.* my soul. *Comp.* Ps. xvi. 9, "my glory," and Macbeth's "mine eternal jewel."

Ver. 21. *yea, from the horns . . .* A sudden rise of believing confidence.

Ver. 26. *shall eat and be satisfied,* i.e. shall thrive. *let your heart revive.* *Comp.* lxix. 32.

Ver. 27. *shall remember*, viz. God (ix. 17).

Ver. 29-31. *Comp.* cii. 16-18. *the fat ones . . .*, i.e. those in the full vigour of life (as xcii. 14), opposed to the feeble shades in Hades. *the dust,* i.e. Hades (*see* on ver. 15). Jehovah's covenant embraces the living and the dead ; *comp.* Phil. ii. 10.

Ver. 30. Even if the present generation should die out, there is the comfort that the next will be able to represent it in the service of Jehovah.

PSALM XXIII. Any pious Israelite's prayer. The "foes" in ver. 5 are national foes (*comp.* iii. 6), and the shepherd's tending is "for his name's sake" (Jehovah, the God of Israel).

Ver. 1. *my shepherd.* For the "good Shepherd" does not neglect the individual (John x. 3, Matt. xviii. 12).

Ver. 2. *waters of resting-places,* i.e. where one may rest. Is the writer thinking of the oases in the desert?

Ver. 3. *the right tracks*, where there are no hindrances.

Ver. 4. *the valley of deadly shade.* In the poem of Job

(xxxviii. 17) "deadly shade" (*i.e.* Hades) is a city with gates. The figure of the shepherd seems to have led to this unusual representation of Hades as a valley. In Ps. xlix. 14 Death himself is pictured as a shepherd; but the good shepherd (like Horus in the Egyptian Elysium) tends his own sheep even in Hades. *thy club and thy staff.* The club to keep off wild beasts; the staff to guide.

Ver. 5. *a table.* A new figure, that of a host.

Ver. 6. *and I shall dwell* See on xxvii. 4.

PSALM XXIV. There is only an artificial connection between the two parts of the psalm. The one is a description of the righteous man (*comp.* Ps. xv.); the other seems to have been composed for the solemn entrance of the ark into the ancient but newly conquered fortress (2 Sam. vi.).

Ver. 7. *Lift up your heads* ... The gates seem too low for the majesty of the great king.

Ver. 12. *Jehovah Sabáoth* = Jehovah God of Sabáoth (the hosts of heaven and of Israel). The phrase, in its abbreviated form, seems to have specially characterized the age of David.

PSALM XXV. An alphabetic psalm (not quite perfect, however), consisting of an appeal to Jehovah's compassion, interrupted by a few verses (8-10, 12-14) in the didactic style. The last verse, which forms an appendix, suggests that the appeal proceeds from Israel personified.

Ver. 3. *vainly. Comp.* ii. 1, 2 Sam. i. 22.

Ver. 11. *for it is great*, so great as to weigh me down.

Ver. 14. *the secret*, viz. either of his government or of his law. *and his covenant* ... Understand, is designed; or explain, his secret and his covenant are designed for their instruction.

PSALM XXVI. Ver. 3. *in thy truthfulness*, i.e. ever conscious of it.

Ver. 6. *I wash my hands*, i.e. I keep them free from sin. *compass thine altar*, either in order to offer the sacrifice, or as a solemn act of thanksgiving (such as was customary later at the Feast of Booths or Tabernacles).

Ver. 12. Faith anticipates the answer to prayer. *on even ground*, a figure for prosperity.

EXPLANATIONS.

PSALM XXVII. Two complete psalms have here been arbitrarily joined together.

Ver. 4. *that I may dwell* . . . How this is possible, is an enigma for the faithful. The solution is, that he who worships God "in spirit and in truth" in the temple will find himself in God's house wherever he is. *pleasantness*, i.e. graciousness, as Ps. xc. 17.

PSALM XXVIII. Ver. 2. *to thy holy chancel*. The phrase describes the innermost part of the sanctuary, the "holy of holies" (1 Kings vi. 16, A.V. oracle).

PSALM XXIX. The glory of Israel's God displayed in the storm, the course of which is traced from Lebanon in the north to Kadesh in the south.

Ver. 1. *sons of God*, i.e. angels (as lxxxix. 6).
Ver. 2. *in hallowed pomp*, i.e. in festival attire.
Ver. 3. *over the waters*, i.e. "the waters that are above the heavens" (Ps. cxlviii. 4).
Ver. 9. *in his palace*, i.e. in heaven (xi. 4, xviii. 6).
Ver. 10. *above the flood*, i.e. either the deluge or the heavenly ocean already referred to in ver. 3.

PSALM XXX. Ver. 1. *drawn me up*, viz. from Hades (ver. 3, *comp.* lxxxviii. 4), or from a "sea of troubles" (*comp.* xviii. 16, lxix. 1, 2).

Ver. 4. *memorial*, i.e. name (as xcvii. 12).
Ver. 5. A "moment" is opposed to "a life," as an "evening" to a "morning." Grief is but a moment in a life-time of God's favour.
Ver. 8. *did I cry*, i.e. when trouble came.

PSALM XXXI. In the style of Jeremiah and the Lamentations. *Comp.* especially ver. 13 (lines 1 and 2) with Jer. xx. 10. The phrase "a dread (is) on every side" occurs six times in Jeremiah.

Ver. 5. *into thy hand*, i.e. into thy providential care.
Ver. 6. *lying vanities*, i.e. idols, as contrasted with the "truthful God" (ver. 5).
Ver. 9. *Have pity* . . . . Faith grounded on past experiences revived the psalmist's courage for a moment. But his sensitive

nature cannot long resist the trials without and within to which it is subjected.

Ver. 15. *My times*, i.e. the crises, the "changes and chances" in my life.

Ver. 20. *the covert of thy face*. The shining of God's face (like brooding wings, lxi. 4) shelters believers from the storms of human passion.

Ver. 21. *in an entrenched city*, i.e. either by protecting me in it when besieged, or by bringing me safely into it (*comp*. lv. 18, line 1). The expression favours a reference to some exceptional event in the speaker's history; similarly the next verse.

PSALM XXXII. Ver. 4. *turned*, "dried up like a potsherd" (xxii. 15).

Ver. 8. *I will instruct thee*. . . . It is uncertain whether Jehovah speaks in this verse (*comp*. xxv. 8, 12), or whether the psalmist (*comp*. xxxiv. 11).

Ver. 10. *pains*, i.e. punishments (Lam. i. 12).

PSALM XXXIII. A collection of twenty-two distichs; the number dictated by that of the Hebrew letters. So Ps. xxxviii., xxxix., cxlvi., Lam. v.

PSALM XXXIV. An imperfectly alphabetic psalm, with a verse added, as in Ps. xxv.

Ver. 6. *This afflicted one*. Not necessarily the psalmist. "This" may mean "yonder"; one out of a number.

Ver. 17. *They cry*, viz. the righteous: certainly not the evildoers, as the common arrangement of the verses would imply.

PSALM XXXV. Ver. 1. *Plead my cause*. . . . A favourite legal figure explained in the next line.

Ver. 10. *All my bones*, i.e. my entire being, both body and soul; *see* on vi. 2.

Ver. 13. *And my prayer* . . . , i.e. Since they are so ungrateful, do thou, O Lord, recompense me in their stead. *into my bosom*, i.e. into the folds of my garment.

Ver. 16. *profane mockers*. Profane, because in mocking at a believer, they do despite to God.

EXPLANATIONS.

PSALM XXXVI. Possibly we have here parts of two psalms, for the connection suggested between ver. 4 and ver. 5 is rather forced.

Ver. 2. *For he flatters him.* It is doubtful whether God or the sinner is the subject. In the latter case render, " For he acts gently towards him."

Ver. 5. Above and around the scenes of the machinations of the wicked, the "philanthropy" of God (Tit. iii. 4) is poured forth.

Ver. 6. *the mountains of God*, the mountains being, above all other objects (except perhaps the trees, civ. 16), monuments of the greatness of the Creator; *comp.* l. 10.

Ver. 7. *the great abyss*, i.e. " the waters under the earth."

Ver. 9. *by thy light* (so xliii. 3). In an Assyrian hymn, the Creator is called " lord of light."

PSALM XXXVII. To be read with Psalm xxxix., lxxiii.; in double verses beginning with the successive letters of the alphabet.

Ver. 3. *the land*, i.e. Palestine, as throughout this psalm.

Ver. 13. *his day*, i.e. the day of the man's death; *comp.* 1 Sam. xxvi. 10, "or his day come that he die."

Ver. 33. *nor condemn him.* . . The world may do so, but Jehovah will pass a different judgment.

Ver. 37. *a posterity.* Lit., "a future," viz. in his descendants. The first immortality conceived of by the Hebrews (as well as by the Greeks) being that of the family.

PSALM XXXVIII. Alphabetic so far as the number of its distichs goes. The speaker is probably suffering Israel personified (*comp.* Lam. iii.). *Comp.* the description of Israel in Isa. i. 5, 6.

Ver. 11. *lovers*, i.e. Israel's friendly neighbours; *comp.* Jer. xxx. 14, Lam. i. 2, 19.

PSALM XXXIX. Ver. 4. *Make me. . to know.* . . Why does the psalmist wish this? That he may not set his hope on earthly goods, but on Him " whose lovingkindness is better than life itself."

Ver. 5. *all is vanity*, i.e. transitory (lit. "a breath").

Ver. 8. *from all my transgressions.* He means from their punishments.

Ver. 12. *a guest,* only a short time here, and dependent on thy protection.

Ver. 13. *that I may gleam again,* i.e. recover my cheerfulness (as Job ix. 27, x. 20).

PSALM XL. Israel personified beseeches God for deliverance.

Ver. 1. *I had waited.* . . Israel calls to mind his mercies in the past, and so strengthens his faith.

Ver. 4. *Happy the man.* . . This and the next verse are not indeed the "new song," but at any rate an echo of it. *treacherously recreant,* probably by apostatizing to heathenism.

Ver. 6. *thou hadst no delight.* Understand, "when Jehovah made a covenant with Israel." *Comp.* Jer. vii. 22, 23. *ears,* i.e. in this connection the faculty of understanding and obeying God's will.

Ver. 7. *Then,* i.e. as soon as my ears were opened. *in the roll of the book,* i.e. the Book of the Law—probably Deuteronomy, in which the "pleasure of Jehovah" is represented as, not a sacrificial ritual, but a well-ordered commonwealth (Deut. iv. 6-8). *it is prescribed,* viz. that I should "work out thy pleasure."

Ver. 9. *righteousness,* i.e. salvation, or the Divine interposition in behalf of Israel (as in the second part of Isaiah).

Ver. 12. *mine iniquities,* i.e. their punishments.

PSALM XLI. Ver. 2. *do not thou.* The change of form shows the strong feeling of the writer.

Ver. 4. The psalmist is one of the "helpless ones" who need "consideration" (ver. 1). But none comes from man. He turns for pity to God.

Ver. 8. The words of the malicious bystanders. His illness, they say, comes from and leads to the realm of "perdition" (*comp.* xviii. 4), it is fixed so fast upon him, that he cannot escape.

Ver. 13. A liturgical addition, *from æon to æon,* i.e. for indefinitely long periods of time. *Comp.* cxlv. 13, "thy kingdom is one of all æons."

Psalms XLII. and XLIII. These two psalms really form but one, as appears from the identity of subject and of refrain, and from the interlacing repetitions. They can only have been separated at a comparatively recent date, as the so-called Psalm xliii. is the only psalm in the Korahite group (xlii.-xlix. unprovided in the Hebrew with a superscription. The author writes at the foot of Mount Hermon, not far from the sources of the river Jordan. Whether he has fled hither from "the oppression of the enemy," or whether he is being carried forcibly to Babylon, is uncertain. A gazelle panting after the fresh streams which descend to the Jordan suggests a happy image for his mood.

Ver. 4. *the throng*, viz. of worshippers going up to the temple at the great festivals.

Ver. 6. *the land of Jordan*, i.e. the land on the eastern side of Jordan. *the hill Mizar*. If the text is correct, some "small" mountain in the N.E. region, now unknown.

Ver. 7. *Flood calls unto floods* .... He compares the sorrows which have seemed to call each other upon him to the waterfalls of the Jordan and its neighbourhood. *thy cataracts.* "Paradise Lost," xi. 824, 5, "all the cataracts Of heav'n set open."

Ver. 8. (*Yet*) *Jehovah will command*. ... The psalmist has two sources of encouragement—one in the past (ver. 4), the other in the future; "Weeping," as another psalmist said, "may endure for a night, but joy cometh in the morning." The day of lovingkindness will dawn again, and even in the night of trouble I can sing my prayers (such as that which follows) to my own personal God. (Or the night may be that which will follow on a day when God has been gracious.) A similar phrase in Job xxxv., 10. *his song*, i.e. a song concerning him. Praise and prayer are not inconsistent ideas (Ps. lxv. ver. 1, 2).

Ver. 1. *a loveless nation*. Want of love and want of common honesty are parallelized as in xii. 1.

Ver. 3. *thy light*. Light stands here for lovingkindness (lvii. 3), being more suitable to the figure of guiding. *bring me*, i.e. bring me again.

Ver. 4. *O God*. Probably, however, we should correct this to Jehovah, as in xlv. ver. 7.

Psalm XLIV. The oppressed, scattered, and insulted Jewish

nation appeals to Jehovah on the ground of its religious fidelity. Probably a Maccabean psalm.

Ver. 5-9. The strange contrast between Israel's deliverances in the past and his present humiliation.

Ver. 12. *Thou sellest* . . . i.e. thou dissolvest thy relation to thy people, *comp.* Deut. xxxii. 30, Isa. lii. 3.

Ver. 19. *therefore*, as a punishment for infidelity. *the place of jackals*, i.e. the desert.

Ver. 22. *for thy sake*, implying that there has been a religious persecution.

PSALM XLV. "A song of lovely things," as the heading in the Hebrew Bible puts it, perhaps with reference to the secondary Messianic sense ascribed to the psalm by those who admitted it into the Psalter. In its historical meaning it is a royal marriage-song. The bride appears from ver. 12 to have been a Tyrian princess; the bridegroom to have been a member of an ancient royal family. Perhaps the psalm refers to the marriage of Joram of Judah and Athaliah (who was of Tyrian blood on her mother's side).

Ver. 2. *Beauteous art thou.* . . . *Comp.* Isa. xxxiii. 17, "the king in his beauty."

Ver. 3. *even thy glory.* The king's sword is the symbol of his glory.

Ver. 4. *for the sake of good faith.* The king is to be the champion of the fundamental civil and religious virtues. He is to protect the faithful as opposed to liars and deceivers, the righteous as opposed to breakers of the law, and the humble as opposed to the proud.

Ver. 8. *out of the ivory palace.* Athaliah was brought up in one (*see* 1 Kings xxii. 39). "Ivory" = adorned with ivory, like the Ninevite palaces. *stringed instruments* . . . . music welcomes the king when he comes to fetch his bride.

Ver. 9. *among thy favourites*, i.e. in the king's own palace, at home.

Ver. 13-18. The queen is described as standing in her bridal array "within," *i.e.* in the women's apartments, and then as conducted in procession to the bridegroom.

Ver. 13. *ouches.* An ouche (Chaucer, nowch; *comp.* niche)

is the frame in which jewels are set. *Comp.* Ex. xxviii. 11 A. V. *unto thee*, viz. the king.

Ver. 16. *in all the earth.* For many peoples will have become the king's loyal subjects (ver. 5, 17). Not only the character (ver. 4, 7) but the fortunes of the king are idealized. Or we might render, "in all the land," *i.e.* throughout the kingdom.

PSALM XLVI. This and the two next psalms seem to have been composed on the same occasion—and not improbably on the overthrow of Sennacherib. The refrain of Ps. xlvi. reminds us of "God (is) with us" in Isa. viii. 8, 10, and Ps. xliii. presents points of contact with Isa. xxxiii.

Ver. 2. *should change*, in fact should "suffer a sea-change."

Ver. 4. Whether a verb has dropped out, or whether the psalmist compares God's lovingkindness to a river, is uncertain. *Comp.* Isa. xxxiii. 21, where Jehovah's protecting presence is likened to "a place of rivers and streams."

Ver. 10. That the danger has been averted is represented as due to a word from God.

PSALM XLVII. Ver. 3, 4. A retrospect of the subjection of the Canaanites and the conquest of Canaan.

Ver. 5. Jehovah's entry into His royal seat on mount Zion, or in the heavenly temple, after a wondrous display of His might.

Ver. 9. A vision of the future (*comp.* cii. 22) is here described as a present fact. *The shields. Comp.* Hos. iv. 18, "her shields" (A. V. her rulers).

PSALM XLVIII. Ver. 2. *Beauteous in elevation.* . . . An echo of Isa. ii. 2, Mic. iv. 1.

Ver. 4. *the kings*, i.e. the Assyrian vassal-kings represented by their generals, or simply the Assyrian generals, "altogether kings" (Isa. x. 8). *combined.* "Paradise Lost," ii. 750, "with them combin'd In bold conspiracy."

Ver. 5. *they saw it*, viz. Jerusalem. But the Hebrew has simply "they saw." The opposite of Cæsar's *veni, vidi, vici.*

Ver. 7. An allegorical description of the overthrow of the Assyrians. *Comp.* Isa xxix. 6, xxxiii. 21.

Ver. 9. *We thought* . . . . referring to the solemn services in the temple during and after the great crisis.

Ver. 12. *Walk about Zion*, viz. to convince yourselves of her safety. Hezekiah's zeal for fortification is mentioned in 2 Chr. xxxii. 5, *comp.* Isa. xxii. 10.

Ver. 14. *for ever and for ever*. A necessary emendation. A. V. renders the received text finely "unto death," Dr. Pusey still more finely "over death" (*comp.* xxiii. 4), but both are against the context, which refers to Israel's fortunes as a nation. The psalmists, like Isaiah and the other prophets, could not accept the idea of the Divine rejection of Israel.

PSALM XLIX. A didactic poem, to console the afflicted believers who formed the Jewish "church" even before the Exile. Hades is not, for them, the end of all things. *Comp.* Ps. lxxiii.

Ver. 7. The context requires this to mean that the rich man *himself* is none the better off for his riches in face of death, and not (as A. V. suggests) that the rich "brother" or kinsman of a dead man is powerless to assist him.

Ver. 11. *Their houses for ever.* Or, "their long homes:" *comp.* Eccl. xii. 5, A. V. "his long home" (or, "his everlasting house"). *in the lands.* Perhaps in the lands which these rich men owned

Ver. 14. *Death is their shepherd.* So in an old Arabic poem ("Hamâsa" ii. 7, 3), "To-day they are driven forward by Death like a troop of camels." *in the morning.* The poor and humble righteous, and these alone, shall have a "morning" after the night of Hades. So Isa. xxvi. 14, "the dead shall not revive;" *ib.* 19, "*thy* dead shall revive." It is an inference from the mystic idea of the believing soul's union with God.

PSALM L. Jehovah judges His people in the presence of "heaven and earth," and sets forth the character and the worship which He requires.

Ver. 1. The accumulation of names (as in Josh. xxii. 22) is to enhance the Divine dignity. *Comp.* Jehovah Elohim (the Lord God, A. V.) in lxxii. 18, Gen. ii., iii., &c.

Ver. 3. *may not* . . . , because the occasion is so great.

Ver. 6. *declare*, i.e. bear witness to.

Ver. 7. *God.* Possibly the original reading was Jehovah.

Ver. 8-15. What the subject of reproof is not, viz. the animal sacrifices of the Jews. It is absurd to honour Jehovah by offering Him a part of His own property; and "if He were hungry," how could He endure such gross nourishment? The acceptable sacrifices are praise and prayer. *Comp.* li. 16, 17.

Ver. 16-21. What the subject of reproof is, viz. the neglect of the simplest moral duties.

Ver. 23. *the way*, i.e. God's way (as xxv. 8).

PSALM LI. A prayer for pardon and sanctification, concluding with a petition for the prosperity of Jerusalem. Whether the last two verses belonged to the psalm from the first, or not, it is clear from the whole tenor of the work that the speaker represents the pious kernel of the people of Israel.

Ver. 4. *Against thee, thee only.* . . . Israel was not, like the Assyrians and Babylonians, an offender against the common rights of nations. Jehovah alone could accuse him; but the history of the past showed how early Israel's defection had begun (*comp.* xxv. 7, Isa. xliii. 27).

Ver. 7. *with hyssop.* A figure from the legal rite of purification by means of a bunch of hyssop.

Ver. 11. *thy holy spirit. Comp.* Isa. lxiii. 10, 11.

Ver. 14. *from blood-guiltiness.* For the old Jerusalem was "full of bloodshed," say the prophets (Isa. i. 15, Mic. iii. 10).

Ver. 18, 19. These verses do not connect well with what precedes; at any rate, the connection is subtle and unoriginal. They were evidently added by an afterthought. Perhaps some other verses once followed ver. 17, which have dropped out of the text.

PSALM LII. Addressed to some high official who misused his power, and is threatened somewhat as Isaiah threatened Shebna (Isa. xxii. 17, 18).

PSALM LV. There is one passage which seems to point to the troubles of an individual, but the greater part of the psalm suggests that the opposition is that of one party to another, and that the speaker is the representative of the humble and righteous but oppressed believers who formed the "church" within the Jewish nation.

Ver. 7. *flit. Comp.* "He that oft-times flitteth," "Thou

tellest my flittings," Prov. xxvii. 8, Ps. lvi. 8, in the Bible of 1551.

Ver. 9. *Swallow up*, i.e. annihilate, as xxi. 9, xxxv. 25. *divide their speech* (lit. their tongue), *i.e.* bring dissension among them (*comp.* Gen. xi. 7).

Ver. 10. *they make their rounds*, viz. to spy out opportunities for evil-doing.

Ver. 11. *from its forum.* Lit. "from its broad place."

Ver. 12-14. A digression, referring to some event in the personal history of the psalmist himself.

Ver 20. A fresh description of the wicked and appeal to Jehovah begins here.

PSALM LVI. Ver. 4. *Through God*, through God's fidelity to his promise.

Ver. 7. *the peoples.* Heathen nations, then, are the enemies referred to.

Ver. 8. *My wanderings.* . . . Each day of my wandering life has been recorded by thee. The psalmist speaks as a persecuted fugitive.

PSALM LVII. Ver. 1. *the destruction*, i.e. the danger of destruction.

Ver. 2. *the Strong One.* The psalmist does not reject the truth he finds in heathen religion; so he retains the common Semitic name of God (El).

Ver. 4. It is not a literally accurate description which follows; hence *with my soul*, i.e. my inward feeling is as if, &c.

PSALM LVIII. Ungodliness and wrong have made such progress in the earth, that the psalmist cannot but ascribe it to supernatural agency. The "gods" or "sons of the most High" (lxxxii. 6) to whom a part of the world's government has been entrusted have neglected their duties, and even helped forward the cause of wickedness. The psalm begins with an angry address to these high powers.

Ver. 2. *ye weigh out.* . . . Ye are as accurate in injustice as ye ought to be in administering justice.

Ver. 9. *Before your pots.* . . . Before your plans are ripe, He will burn up you and your devices. The picture is that of a fire in an Oriental village. The thorns have to be kindled; then, when the fire has burned up, the caldrons are put on. But before the pots with the flesh can feel the fire in the thorns, they are swept away by a whirlwind.

Ver. 11. The abounding iniquity tempted men to atheism. But now these providential interpositions force even heathens to confess that *there are divine powers* (Elohim) *that judge* (justly) *in the earth*.

PSALM LIX. *Comp.* Ps. lv. The speaker is a representative pious Israelite.

Ver. 11. *Slay them not.* Let them be living monuments of retributive justice.

PSALM LX. A prayer after a grievous defeat. Israel personified encourages himself by thinking of an ancient word of promise.

Ver. 4. *Thou hast given a banner.* . . . The cause is that of the true God. He has, as it were, given them the banner; but instead of serving as a rallying-point, this strange sort of flag has only led them to their ruin. There is a play upon the words "banner" and "flee," in the original.

Ver. 6. *let me exult.* The psalmist exults, and appropriates the details of the Divine promise. *Shechem* and *Succoth*, the one on the west, the other on the east, of Jordan, represent the territory of N. Israel, which appears to be exposed to more danger than that of Judah.

Ver. 8. Israel's three most troublesome neighbours are defied. *will I cast out my shoe*, i.e. assign the lot of subjugation.

Ver. 9. *the entrenched city*, i.e. perhaps the rock-built city, Petra.

PSALM LXI. Ver. 2. *From the end of the earth*, i.e. from some distant region.

Ver. 4. *for ever;* lit. for æons, *i.e.* for an indefinitely long period, for an eternity like that of Jehovah (Isa. xl. 28).

Ver. 5. *hast hardened*, viz. in time past.

PSALM LXII. Some pious Israelite of high rank is in imminent danger from malignant opponents, and encourages himself and his companions to hold fast to their faith.

The last four verses are in a different key.

Ver. 10. A warning to the pious amidst their temptations. Simple faith and obedience is the only trustworthy resource. The terms *perverseness* and *crookedness* show the influence of the " wise men" and their proverbs. *If riches increase* . . . , *comp.* xlix. 16.

Ver. 11. *God hath spoken once* . . . "Once" and "twice" in parallel clauses mean "again and again" (Job xxxiii. 14, xl. 5). The psalmist claims for himself (and therefore for all believers) a subjective conviction of certain fundamental truths, produced by the Divine Spirit (*comp.* lxxxv. 8). On this warrant he once more proclaims the old truth, that power belongs only to God, but supplements it directly by a less generally recognized truth, that the God who reveals Himself in Israel (*i.e.* Jehovah) is also essentially kind, that instead of crushing frail man for his "lapses" (xix. 12), He will reward him according to his work, *i.e.* in proportion to his honest endeavours to serve God. For this wide view of "revelation," *comp.* Job iv. 12-21, xxxiii. 14-16, Joel ii. 28-29.

PSALM LXIII. The circumstances described are similar to those in Ps. lxi. ; *comp.* also Ps. xlii. xliii.

Ver. 1. *my flesh*, i.e. my body (*comp.* xvi. 9). *fainting land.* There is an implied figure like that of the gazelle in xlii. 1.

Ver. 2. *In such wise*, i.e. because thou art my God, and I seem so far from thee and thy temple (like lxi. 2, xlii. 2). *in the sanctuary*, because there in time past " service high and anthem clear" could "bring all heav'n before mine eyes."

Ver. 3. Meantime, severed though he is from the material sanctuary, his heart has become a temple of praise. His "longing" is satisfied: he has solved the enigma of xxvii. 4 (*see note*). All this must be imagined, before we can understand the transition from the melancholy of the first to the ecstatic joy of the second stanza.

Ver. 4. *In such wise*, i.e. because by a moment's "earnest seeking," I have found thee—in my heart's temple, in mystic union with the God of love.

Ver. 9. Like the Scotch Covenanters, the psalmist has no

sense of incongruity between deeply spiritual musings, and vehement denunciations of his enemies. *His* enemies are those who would frustrate God's purposes for Israel.

PSALM LXIV. Sin brought punishment; but Jehovah has restored comparative security to His people, and has "crowned" his benefits with an abundant crop of ripening corn. It is a bright idea to connect this psalm with the end of the period of disturbance caused by the invasion of Sennacherib, when the fields were again adorned with ripening corn (Isa. xxxvii. 30).

Ver. 2. *let all flesh come.* A longing for the time of which Isaiah prophesied in ii. 2, 3. *Comp.* ver. 5, 8.

Ver. 3. *Guilty deeds* ... The psalmist is oppressed by the consciousness of national sins (*comp.* xxxviii. 4).

Ver. 4. *With terrible things* ... Such, for instance, as the destruction of Sennacherib's army.

Ver 5. *the confidence* ... The wonderful history of Israel (such is the faith of the psalmist) has impressed the nations first of all with fear (ver. 8) and then with confidence.

Ver. 7. *and the tumult of the peoples.* No mere casual poet's phrase. *Comp.* xlvi. 3, 6 (still more plausibly ascribed to the period after Sennacherib's overthrow) with Isa. xvii. 12-14.

Ver. 8. *the ends*, viz. of the earth (ver. 5); in other words, east and west, *the sources of morning and evening.* "Morning" and "evening" are here synonyms for the sun, who "goes forth" from the east and "goes in" at the west.

Ver. 9. *the river of God*, i.e. the water stored up behind the "doors" and "lattices" of heaven (lxxviii. 23, Gen. vii. 11). *thus fully*, i.e. with the overflow of God's inexhaustible river.

Ver. 11. *The year of thy goodness*, i.e. the year so full of thy good gifts. *thy tracks*, as though Jehovah drove through the land in His chariot, not as a man of war (as Hab. iii.), but to scatter the blessings of peace.

Ver. 13. *they shout for joy*, i.e. the meadows and valleys. When the seed sown brings forth a hundredfold (Gen. xxvi. 12), it is not enough to speak of "smiling fields."

PSALM LXVI. A singular contrast with Ps. li ! The psalmist is a prayerful man, and echoes (we might say, popularizes) the prophetic idea of the world-wide significance of Israel's history. But his closing thoughts are those of personal innocence and material sacrifice. As in Ps. li. and so many other psalms, the singer represents the church-nation of Israel.

Ver. 6. *there let us rejoice in him.* The speaker identifies himself with the Israelites of the Exodus. But it is very possible that the text is inaccurate or incomplete.

Ver. 11. *into the hold,* i.e. into subjection to a foreign power. *laidest a crushing weight,* i.e. didst treat us like beasts of burden.

Ver. 12. *mortal men* ... Elsewhere Israel is encouraged by the thought of the mortal nature of its tyrants (Isa. li. 12); here, however, it is the ignominy of servitude, to be tyrannized over by the creatures of a day. *fire ... water,* images for the varieties of deadly peril.

Ver. 13. Instead of merging himself in the people, the speaker now apparently merges the people in himself. Possibly he is the high priest; possibly the poet rises into personification.

Ver. 14. *Such as escaped* ... Extorted by the necessity of the moment, like the vow of Jephthah (Judg. xi. 35, 36, same word).

Ver. 17. *was (already) under my tongue.* So confident was he of an answer.

Ver. 18, 19. A reassuring inference from recent events as to the moral state of the people. God never hears the prayer of the wicked. But God has lately given a striking answer to prayer; Israel, therefore, is "absolved from great transgression" (xix. 13).

Ver. 20. *my prayer,* i.e. that for which I prayed.

PSALM LXVII. A prayer that God will bless Israel in order that men may be attracted to Israel's God. An abundant harvest gives ground for hoping that God *will* grant the wide-reaching prayer. The opening words are an adaptation of the words of the priestly blessing, Numb. vi. 24-26.

PSALM LXVIII. Dante's contemporary, and the friend of Dante's friends, the Rabbi and poet Immanuel, in his Hebrew journey through Paradise, sees king David surrounded by the most learned commentators, to whom he propounds the riddle of the lxviiith psalm. Immanuel's solution alone wins the sweet psalmist's approval. King David, however, cannot really be the psalmist, since the temple is referred to in ver. 29, the dispersion in ver. 22, the Samaritans indirectly in ver. 27, the hostility of Egypt and other nations whom the Jews are described as without power to assist, in ver. 30 ; and the whole work is so full of allusions to other psalms that we cannot help referring it to the post-Exile period. Many psalms, no doubt, can be fairly well understood without fixing their date, but certainly not the lxviiith. And yet, artificial as it is, how strong is the lyric emotion which pervades the whole, and makes it live ! All the feelings, recollections, hopes, and anticipations of the age have found in it an adequate expression.

Ver. 1. The psalm opens with the chant with which the ark set forward in the wilderness (Numb. x. 35).

Ver. 4. *cast up a way*, as pioneers for a royal progress, Isa. xl. 3. *through the deserts*, alluding to the Divine guidance of the Israelites either from Egypt or from Babylonia to the promised land.

Ver. 6. *the rebellious*, i.e. primarily the Israelites who perished in the wilderness.

Ver. 7, 8. A retrospect, borrowed from Judges v. 4, 5, of the journey through the wilderness. Jehovah leaves His seat upon mount Sinai, and marches before His people. *Comp.* Deut. xxxiii. 2, Hab. iii. 3.

Ver. 9, 10. Meantime supernatural powers are at work, preparing the promised land for Israel's reception. To enhance the effect, Canaan is described as fainting, weary, and dry before it became Jehovah's inheritance. *Comp.* Gen. xlvii. 13, "The land of Canaan fainted by reason of the famine." *Thy living creatures.* They were so "poor"—but just alive ; God's "animals" (so Vulgate).

Ver. 11-14. The victories of the period of the Judges. The stanza may be partly made up of fragments of ancient songs, and hence its obscurity.

Ver. 15-18. At last Jehovah has found a dwelling-place. The honour is not for the peaks of Bashan (though "mountains of God" in respect of size), but for Zion. Surrounded by His "chariots of victory" (Hab. iii. 8), and carrying with him His captives, Jehovah ascends to His throne. The "captives" are also "gifts"—they have surrendered of themselves (*comp.* Isa. xlv. 14); once they were "rebellious"

Ver. 19-23. Here the second part of the psalm begins. Israel sustains himself in perilous times by doxologies and prophecies of vengeance.

Ver. 22. A Divine oracle. Jehovah's enemies will not be safe even in the woods and glens of Bashan, or the depths of the ocean.

Ver. 24-27. A description of a festival procession. The transition is abrupt, and the opening words are vague. Possibly something has fallen out of the text.

Ver. 26. *of the fountain of Israel*, i.e. true Israelites; *comp.* Isa. xlviii. 1.

Ver. 27. The tribes mentioned are those which constituted Judæa and Galilee, the two orthodox provinces of the post-Exile period.

Ver. 28-31. The psalmist, then, is grateful for the past, but he longs for a fuller accomplishment of the prophecies. In symbolical language he refers to the rival dynasties of the Ptolemies and the Seleucidæ, who, with their greedy mercenaries, contend for the possession of Canaan, to the sore disquieting of Israel.

PSALM LXIX. *Comp.* Ps. xxii., xxxv., cii.

Ver. 25. *encampment . . . tents.* Here used in the general sense of "dwelling."

PSALM LXXI. Little more than a cento of phrases from other psalms, such as xxii., xxxi., xxxv., xl., &c.

Ver. 7. *as a prodigy*, because I have escaped so many dangers.

Ver. 15. *the numbers thereof. Comp.* xl. 5, cxxxix. 17, 18.

PSALM LXXII. Prayers and idealizing anticipations on the accession of a crown prince.

Ver. 1. *thy judgments*, i.e. judgments as righteous as thine.

Ver. 3. *May the mountains . . . Comp.* the parallel in Isa. xlv. 8.

Ver. 10. *Sheba*, i.e. S. Arabia. *Seba*, i.e. the Ethiopian island and city of Meroe.

Ver. 16. *upon the top of the mountains*, i.e. on the terraces which cover the lofty slopes of Lebanon. *like Lebanon*, stately and multitudinous.

PSALM LXXIII. *Comp.* Ps. xxxvii., xlix. But this psalm is superior from the tenderness of its piety.

Ver. 6. *no tortures*, no agonies of pain or grief.

Ver. 7. *caul.* See on xvii. 10.

Ver. 8. *from on high*, as if he were a god; lit. *from the (heavenly) height.*

Ver. 10. *his people*, i.e. weak-minded Israelites, who are tempted to fall away; his = their. The following verses describe their self-deluding argument.

Ver. 20. *their semblance*, i.e. their unsubstantial, phantom-life. *Comp.* Ps. xxxix. 7.

Ver. 24. *afterward*, i.e. after death? or after the sleep of Hades?

Ver. 25. The highest "sons of God" have no interest for him; and "to which of the holy ones should he turn?" (Job v. 1.)

Ver. 26. *should have wasted away*, i.e. should seem to have wasted away.

PSALM LXXIV. *Comp.* the prayer of Judas Maccabeus, 2 Macc. viii. 2-4.

Ver. 4. *their signs*, i.e. the emblems and rites of heathen religion—Zeus substituted for Yahveh (Jehovah). *Comp.* 1 Macc. i. 54.

Ver. 8. *Their family altogether* . . . 1 Macc. i. 50, "And whosoever would not do according to the commandment of the king, he should die." (*Comp.* lxxxiii. 4.) But "to kill the body" would be too long an undertaking; "to kill the soul"—or the nerve of the spiritual life—would be a shorter and not less effectual way of putting out the light of Israel. Hence *all God's places of meeting*, i.e. all the synagogues, are burned up.

Ver. 9. *our signs.* In contrast to "their signs," ver. 4. *no prophet.* This was the great complaint of the Maccabean period. *Comp.* 1 Macc. iv. 46, ix. 27, xiv. 41.

Ver. 13, 14. *the dragons . . . leviathan.* Synonymous symbolic expressions for Egypt. *See* for the former, Isa. li. 9, Ezek.

xxix. 3, xxxii. 2. Leviathan = wreathed. *gavest him to be food.* ... i.e. gavest the dead bodies of the Egyptians to be a prey to the tribes of wild beasts. So the ants and rock-badgers are called a people in Prov. xxx. 25, 26.

Ver. 15. An allusion to the miracles of the water from the rock, and the passage of the Jordan.

Ver. 16. *the light-bearer.* In Gen. i. 16 the sun and moon both receive this name; here, as it seems, the moon alone.

PSALM LXXV. Thanksgiving. Ver. 2-5. A divine revelation which consoled the pious in their extremity. "Jehovah will seize the right opportunity to do justice. The earth is in a state of alarm; but needlessly so, for its moral supports are 'adjusted,' arranged with a nice eye to the fabric they are to bear, by Jehovah, and boastfulness and impiety shall meet with a check."

Ver. 6-8. Help and Justice come from God alone, who disposes of the destinies of the nations. *the mountainous desert,* i.e. the south.

PSALM LXXVI. Thanksgiving for the overthrow either of the Assyrians, or (in the Maccabean period) of the Seleucid Syrians.

Ver. 5. *have lost their hands.* Comp. Josh. viii. 20, "they had no hand (A. V. power) to flee this way or that."

Ver. 10. God's wrath is inexhaustible. After each fresh outburst there is still a *residue* to gird Himself with for a fresh battle.

PSALM LXXVII. The psalmist recalls some dark moments he has lately had; perhaps even quotes the psalm in which he expressed his struggle against despair. He describes how he recovered his balance by remembering God's mercies in ancient times (so that national mercies are meant, and therefore national troubles).

Verses 16-19, descriptive of a theophany, seem to be a variation upon Hab. iii. 10-15. How they came into their present place, is an enigma.

Ver. 2. *stretched forth,* i.e. in supplication, as xxviii. 2.

Ver. 4. *the guards of mine eyes,* i.e. mine eyelids.

Ver. 10. *It is my sickness*, i.e. my chastening from God. Understand, "but let me not despair." Then follows an elevating thought expressed in its simplest form like an exclamation, *the years*, &c.

Ver. 13. *Holiness* has, at any rate here, no ethical tinge; it is correlative to "greatness," and is displayed in wonderful works. Practically it means uniqueness, with the secondary idea of unapproachableness (*Comp.* 1 Sam. vi. 20).

Ver. 15. *Joseph* is mentioned as the ancestor of Ephraim and Manasseh.

PSALM LXXVIII. Ver. 9. The expressions are metaphorical (*comp.* ver. 57). Ephraim's failure is mentioned, not as though Judah had been more successful, but to prepare the way for the rejection of Shiloh and Ephraim in ver. 60, 67.

Ver. 25. *The food of the Mighty*, i.e. of the angels.

PSALM LXXIX. Another undoubtedly Maccabean psalm.

Ver. 2. *Comp.* 1 Macc. vii. 16, "Howbeit he took of them [the Assidaioi] three-score men, and slew them in one day, according to the words which he wrote (Ps. lxxix. 2). *thy loving ones.* The same word (khasidim) under the form *Assidaioi*, became a party-name in the Maccabean times (*see* 1 Macc. ii. 42).

PSALM LXXX. On the incomplete restoration of the Jews.

Ver. 2. Judah prays that her neighbour Benjamin and the great northern tribes may be brought back to strengthen her against the hostile Samaritans.

Ver. 5. *in large measures*, i.e. in vessels larger than ordinary cups.

Ver. 17. *the man ... the son of man*, i.e. the Israelitish people.

PSALM LXXXI. Two fragments of psalms, the former of which ends and the latter begins with the Exodus, but which have nothing else in common.

Ver. 3. The *festal day* spoken of is the passover (see ver. 5), which was celebrated at the full moon of the month Nisan. Apparently the new moon at the beginning of this month, as well as the full moon, was marked by the blowing of trumpets.

Ver. 5. *when he went forth*, viz. Jehovah (*comp.* Ex. xi. 4, 5). *of one I had not known*. A mysterious way of expressing the supernatural nature of the speaker (*comp.* Job iv. 16).

Ver. 6. *the basket*, viz. that in which the Israelites conveyed clay or baked bricks. *my thunder-covert;* compare xviii. 12. The special allusion, however, is to the pillar of cloud at the passage of the Red Sea (Ex. xiv. 19, 20).

PSALM LXXXII. *Comp.* Ps. lviii. The patron-angels of the nations are accused of permitting violence and injustice, so that the moral bases of the earth are shaken. They are threatened, divine as they are, with the one great evil common to princes and peasants alike.

PSALM LXXXIII. Most of the nations mentioned in ver. 6-8 appear in 1 Macc. v. as enemies of the Jews, and the psalm may be plausibly regarded as Maccabean. Amalek and Assyria (or should we read *Geshur?*), however, seem anachronisms.

PSALM LXXXIV. *Comp.* Ps. xlii., lxiii.

Ver. 3. The psalmist looks back with longing regret to his happy times of communion with God in the temple. There was his heart's true home.

Ver. 6. *the balsam-vale.* Comp. 2 Sam. v. 22-25, where the *bācā*, a kind of balsam-tree, is spoken of as in the valley of Refaim, N.W. of Jerusalem. A tree with the same name grows in the barren valley of Mecca. Whether some well-known route to Jerusalem led through a valley so called, or whether it is a typical expression for a dry valley, is uncertain. *they make it* . . . Reminding us of Isa. xxxv. 7 xli. 18, only those belong to prophecies of the blissful outward condition of the Jews after the Return, whereas this describes the inward subjective miracles wrought by faith. The *early rain* is equally metaphorical.

Ver. 7. *They go* . . . i.e. they have continual supplies of grace; *comp.* John i. 16.

Ver. 9. *thine anointed*, i.e. either the king, or the high priest, if the psalm be Maccabean.

PSALM LXXXV. A combination of two contrasting parts (*comp.* Ps. cxxvi.). It seemed at first as if God's anger were removed, but there is still too much need to pray, "Return to us." Jehovah answers with words of peace (*comp.* on lxii. 11).

PSALM LXXXVII. The conversion of the heathen, one of the "honourable things," or privileges, of Messianic Jerusalem. *Comp.* ver. 4 with Isa. xix. 18-25, xlv. 19, and ver. 5, 6 (*born in her, born there*) with Isa. xliv. 5.

PSALM LXXXVIII. The most melancholy of all the psalms. Many of its thoughts and phrases remind us of the book of Job, and the hopeless view of the next life recalls the psalm of Hezekiah. The speaker is apparently an individual, but may be, as so often, a personification of the Jewish people.

Ver. 11. *in Abaddon.* Milton well, "in perdition." Notice how Abaddon is introduced in Job xxvi. 6, xxviii. 22, Rev. ix. 11.

Ver. 15. *even from youth.* So Israel in Ps. cxxix. 1, "from my youth up."

PSALM LXXXIX. The contrast between the ancient promises to David's house and the present lot of the heirs of those promises.

Ver. 3, 4. For the covenant, *see* 2 Sam. vii. 5-17.

Ver. 7. *the council of holy ones*, synonymous with "the council of God" (Jer. xxiii. 18, Job xv. 8), such a council as is described in Job i. 6, ii. 2. The "holy ones" are the angels, as Job v. 1, xv. 15.

Ver. 15. *the glad shouting*, i.e. of those who rejoice at some great national deliverance.

Ver. 18. Israel's *shield* (or defender, *comp.* xlvii. 9), or, in simpler style, his *king*, belongs to Jehovah. He is therefore sacrosanct, inviolable.

Ver. 19-37. The promises of 2 Sam. vii. are reproduced more in detail, and here and there with even heightened colours; *in a vision*, refers to 2 Sam. vii. 17.

Ver. 37. *the witness in the sky.* God, the moon, and the rainbow have all been thought of, but at the close of the speech an appeal to Jehovah seems most in point (*comp.* Job. xvi. 19).

Ver. 50. *the reproach of peoples.* Comp. Ezek. xxxvi. 15, "neither shalt thou bear the reproach of peoples any more."

Ver. 51. *the footsteps of thine anointed,* i.e. wherever he goes.

PSALM XC. Contemplations on the shortness of life as contrasted with God's eternity, and on the connection of death and sin, leading up to petitions for the restoration of God's favour to his long humiliated people. Ver. 7, 9 make it probable that an extraordinary mortality prevailed when the psalm was written.

Ver. 1. *from age to age.* Israel then is no longer a young nation.

Ver. 2. *from æon to æon,* one æon (see lxi. 4, note) extending indefinitely in the past, and the other in the future.

Ver. 6. Mankind, like the grass, is continually renewed only to be as continually destroyed.

Ver. 11. *Who hath learned* . . . Who has realized the intensity of God's displeasure against sin in the degree which "the fear of God" (i.e. true religion) requires?

Ver. 17. *let the pleasantness* . . . May we be encompassed with sensible tokens of the divine favour! *over us,* as xxxiii. 22

PSALM XCI. Ver. 13. By a sudden and effective transition Jehovah becomes the speaker.

PSALM XCIII. Ver. 5. *thy testimonies,* i.e. thy declarations, or, more specially, thy commands (xix. 7). *holiness,* i.e. inviolability.

PSALM XCIV. Ver. 15. *for judgment* . . . judgment, now so much abused by those who are charged with it, *must turn again* and join itself to *righteousness.*

Ver. 17. *Silence,* a synonym for Hades, as cxv. 17, *comp.* xxxi. 17.

PSALM XCV. Ver. 1-7*a*. The psalmist encourages his countrymen to the joyous and thankful worship of Jehovah.

Ver. 7*b*-11. Another psalmist implores Israel not to shut his ears to the warning oracle. *saw my work*, i.e. my judicial work, as xxviii. 5.

PSALMS XCVI.-XCVIII. Israel's hope—the direct revelation of Jehovah as Governor of the world. Reminiscences of second part of Isaiah abound.

PSALM XCVII. Ver. 12. *memorial = name*, as xxx. 4, cxxxv. 13, &c.

PSALM XCIX. Ver. 6-8. Instances of the justice of Jehovah's rule. For Moses as a priest, *see* Ex. xxiv., xl. 22-27, Lev. viii.

PSALM CI. Resolutions of an Israelitish ruler of uncertain date. Ver. 2. *when wilt thou come unto me?* Isa. lxiv. 5, "Thou meetest . . . those who remember thee in thy ways."
Ver. 3. *deeds that swerve*, i.e. from the standard of uprightness.

PSALM CII. This psalm is full of allusions, and from internal evidence cannot have been composed before the latter part of the Exile. But though an elegiac, it is not a penitential psalm. The phraseology points partly to an individual, partly to the nation as the subject. But, as we have seen already, individualizing passages may occur in a strictly national psalm.
Ver. 5. An allusion to Job xix. 20. "Skin and flesh" is an inexact expression, inserted to fill out the line; in Lam. iv. 8 "flesh" is omitted.
Ver. 24. The nation speaks. Its continuance is guaranteed by the everlastingness of its God (as so often said in ii. Isaiah).

PSALM CIII. The first part of a great hymn to Providence, treating of God's mercies to personified Israel. For the imagery, *comp.* Isa. xl. 6-8, 22, 26, 31.
Ver. 1. *my soul*. The substratum of man (his personality) is put for the man himself; hence we need not wonder at the expressions in ver. 4, 5. So in cv. 18, Joseph's "soul" is described as put in fetters.

Ver. 20-21. Jehovah Sabáoth means, to this psalmist, Jehovah the God of armies. The angels are God's "mighty ones" (as Joel iii. 11). During and after the Exile, the thoughts of the Jews were much turned towards the angels, who seemed to bridge over the gulf between the awful Creator and the children of men.

PSALM CIV. The preceding psalm had no adequate conclusion; ver. 19*b* strikes the key-note for Ps. civ.—the second part of the hymn to Providence. Man is not included in this poetical version of the first of Genesis, because this part of creation was treated of in Ps. ciii. Only in the closing words is one portion of humanity referred to—the sinners "o'erpowering with harsh din" the harmony of creation. So that in reality we have here only the five days represented; the verses which should be given to the sixth are occupied by the providential feeding of all living things (ver. 27-30). The poetical beauties are greatest in the description of the third day's work. There is a striking parallel to them in the praises of the Providence of the Egyptian sun-god (Amen-ka), transl. Goodwin, *Records of the Past*, ii. 132-3.

> " maker of grass for the cattle,
> fruitful trees for men;
> causing the fish to live in the river;
> the birds to fill the air
>
> *   *   *   *   *   *
>
> providing food for the rats in their holes;
> feeding the flying things in every tree."

Ver. 7, 8. The appearance of the dry land when *the mountains rose* into view.

Ver. 16. *The trees of Jehovah*, i.e. planted by him (as Numb. xxiv. 6). *See* on xxxvi. 6.

Ver. 17, 18. The scene is exactly that still presented near the cedar-grove of Lebanon (A. P. Stanley).

Ver. 26. *there is Leviathan* . . . The title Leviathan ("the coiler") properly belongs to a great serpent (Isa. xxvii. 1); in Job xl. 25 it means the crocodile. Here it designates some monster of the sea. *to sport with him*. Comp. Job xli. 5,

"Wilt thou sport with him as with a bird?" These monsters, so feared by man, are tame and tractable to God.

Ver. 30. Life, not death, is the master-principle of the universe.

PSALM CV. Ver. 15. *mine anointed ones.* As if they were princes. The psalmist involuntarily antedates his own idealizing conception of the patriarchs. Hence, too, the expression, "my prophets," though Abraham, at least, is called a prophet in Gen. xx. 7.

Ver. 19. *his word*, i.e. Joseph's prophetic word, which, at any rate at first, was combined with *the promise of Jehovah* to himself. The delay in the fulfilment of the promise *assayed* or purified his spiritual character.

PSALM CVI. The history of Israel treated from a new point of view—that of the penitent.

Ver. 15. *leanness*, i.e. a wasting disease; *comp.* Isa. x. 16.

Ver. 20. *his glory*, the glory of Jehovah, which they had so often been privileged to see.

Ver. 28. *They yoked themselves* . . .] The phrase used in Numb. xxv. 3. *the dead*, i.e. the idol-gods alluded to in Numb. xxv. 2. *Comp.* Isa. viii. 19.

Ver. 37. *the demons*; lit. the shēdim, the plural of *shēd*, connected with Assyr. *sidu*, a genius or demigod, more particularly the symbolic winged bull placed at the entrances of palaces.

PSALM CVII. A series of picturesque descriptions separated by two refrains, and all exhibiting the contrast between present peace and past tribulation. It is therefore virtually another hymn to Providence. At first, indeed, the psalmist simply intended a thanksgiving for Israel's restoration, but to fill out his poem he included some scenes not connected with that great turning-point. At ver. 33 the treatment becomes more meagre, and the thought less original. The refrains are dropped, and the whole passage was evidently written later, though by the same author.

PSALM CIX. The most startling of the imprecatory psalms. A typical pious Israelite, or perhaps the pious kernel of the nation, complains in bitter terms of malicious enemies, particularly of one of them, high in office, like Sanballat or Tobiah in Nehemiah's time. *Comp.* Nehemiah's imprecations upon Tobiah, Neh. iv. 4, 5.

Ver. 6. *at his right hand,* the place of the accuser.

Ver. 21. *Adonai,* i.e. Lord, exclusively applied to Jehovah.

Ver. 23. *as the locust,* a helpless, unsteady thing ; *comp.* Job xxxix. 20.

PSALM CX. Two Divine oracles addressed to one who is priest and king in one, i.e. either to the Messianic king, as viewed first of all in David's time (*see* 1 Sam. xxiii. 6, 9, 2 Sam. vi. 14-18), and again especially soon after the Restoration (*see* Zech. iii. 8, vi. 11-13), or to the Maccabean high priest. The conclusion is abrupt and perhaps fragmentary.

Ver. 1, 2. The first oracle is in two parts, one describing how Jehovah will clear a space for *my Lord* to rule in, the other how the latter personage is to govern as Jehovah's viceroy.

Ver. 3. The martial young men of Israel second Jehovah and his viceroy with enthusiasm. *The holy mountains,* i.e. the hills about Jerusalem (as lxx::vii. 1), whence the army sets forth. *from the dawn,* from the very dawn of life.

Ver. 4. *a priest for ever.* So of Zadok it was prophesied, "I will build him a sure house, and he (i.e. his family) shall walk before mine anointed for ever" (1 Sam. ii. 35). *after the manner* (not of Aaron and of Zadok, but) *of Melchizedek,* both king and priest (Gen. xiv. 18.)

Ver. 7. A scene from the pursuit of the enemy. *Comp.* 2 Sam. xxiii. 15 (David's longing for the water of Bethlehem).

PSALM CXI. This and the next psalm are alphabetical, each line beginning with one of the twenty-two Hebrew letters.

PSALM CXIII. With this psalm begins the "Egyptian Hallel" (or hymn), which lasts on to the end of Ps. cxviii., and which was recited at the three great feasts, at the New Moons, and at the Feast of Dedication.

PSALM CXVI. National thanksgivings for deliverance from danger.

Ver. 3. *The cords of Death,* the hunter (xviii. 4 note).

Ver. 10. *when thus I spoke,* referring to the supplication in ver. 4.

Ver. 13. *I will take* ..., a ritual act, expressive of gratitude. *salvations,* i.e. manifold or abundant salvation.

PSALM CXVIII. Intended to be sung antiphonally by different singers or choirs on the occasion of some great event in the history of the temple, such as the dedication of the second temple (Ezra vi. 15-18), or its purification by Judas Maccabeus (1 Macc. iv. 52-58).

Ver. 19. This would be spoken by the festal company on reaching the temple-gate; the priests and Levites who receive them would respond in ver. 20. Ver. 26 will also belong to the latter.

Ver. 22. A proverbial expression; the *builders* are the Gentiles, *the head corner stone* (which unites two walls and supports the roof) is the Jewish nation.

Ver. 27. *even unto.* Understand, "and bring it," or "and lift it up (unto)."

PSALM CXIX. Mnemonic book of devotion, in which the eight lines of each division begin with the same letter of the Hebrew alphabet. The subject is the duty and blessedness of the study of the Law. The thought may be monotonous, but there is considerable variety in the expression, or in the grouping of the same familiar phrases. Nor are the sayings always entirely devoid of connection (*see* the 12th stanza and the 13th, Lamed and Mem). The speaker is evidently the Jewish nation personified: the "proud" who oppress him are the persecuting kings of the family of the Seleucidæ. Of course, the reverence here expressed for the law does not exclude a loving study of the works of the prophets, regarded (rightly or wrongly) as continuators of the work of Moses. It is evident, indeed, that the writer has imbibed much of their spirit, as he nowhere refers to the details of rites and ceremonies, and in ver. 108 presents to God "the freewill offerings of his mouth." He is a kindred spirit to the author of Ps. li. (taking in its short but weighty appendix).

Ver. 176. *like a lost sheep.* The distressed condition of Israel is compared to that of sheep left to themselves in the wilderness. *Comp.* Jer. l. 6.

PSALM CXX. This and the next fourteen psalms having the same heading, we may conclude that they once formed a separate collection. What the heading means, is too difficult a question to enter upon here. None of these psalms requires, from internal evidence, to be placed in the pre-Exile period.

Ver. 4. The wrath of Jehovah described in figures from nomad life. *coals of broom*, the roots of which plant are used by the Arabs for charcoal.

Ver. 5. *Meshech* (tribes between the Black and the Caspian Sea) and *Kedar* (the nomad tribes of north Arabia) either represent the remote regions in which the Jews were dispersed, or symbolize the malignant neighbours of the Jews at home in Nehemiah's time.

PSALM CXXI. Ver. 1. *unto the mountains*, i.e. those of Jerusalem (*comp.* lxxxvii. 1, cxxxiii. 3). *whence* . . . The question is asked, not out of weak faith, but in order to give more effect to the answer; *comp.* xxiv. 8.

Ver. 4. Compare, from the Egyptian hymn quoted already—

> " Hail to thee for all these things,
> the One alone with many hands
> lying awake when all men lie (asleep),
> to seek out the good of his creatures."

PSALM CXXV. Ver. 3. *sceptre*, i.e. rule. *rest*, i.e. abide. *lot*, i.e. allotted portion.

PSALM CXXVI. Note the enigmatical contrast between the two parts of the psalm (*see* on Ps. lxxxv.).

Ver. 4. *as the streams* . . . , as the water-courses in the parched *Negeb* (in the south of Palestine) are filled with rushing torrents by the winter rains.

PSALM CXXVII. All good things, from the building of a house to the founding of a family (itself a house, in Hebrew phraseology), depend on the Divine blessing.

Ver. 2. Why spoil God's gift of sleep by over-carefulness?

Ordinary exertions, with God's blessing, will effect far more than the greatest unblessed energy.

> "O earth, so full of dreary noises!
> O men, with wailing in your voices!
> O delvèd gold, the wailers heap!
> O strife, O curse, that o'er it fall!
> God strikes a silence through you all,
> And giveth His beloved sleep."

Ver. 3. *children are a heritage*, not as of legal right, but as a free gift (so the word implies). Like safety, and like sleep, they are the gift of God.

PSALM CXXX. Ver. 4. *that thou mayest be feared.* Forgiveness, according to the psalmists, involves the removal of the temporal punishment of sin. Hence the sight of Israel's forgiveness may bring others to "fear" and worship Jehovah.

PSALM CXXXI. This psalm is in the unwonted key of humility (*comp*. on vii. 8). It is "like a string of a Christian Lyra Innocentium placed among the psaltery's chords out of due season."

PSALM CXXXII. Israel, after the Restoration, longs for the promised ruler of the house of David, and reminds Jehovah of the meritorious conduct of David.

Ver. 3. *tent* is used conventionally for "house."

Ver. 6. Israel, even at this late period, feels itself one with the Israel of David's time, when the ark was transferred from Kirjath-jearim, first to the house of Obed-Edom, and then to Mount Zion. The Israelites, says the psalmist, first of all inquired for the ark in Ephratah, and at last found it at one of the towns of that district (1 Chr. ii. 50), Jaar, i.e. Kirjath-jearim ("the city of woods").

Verses 8-10 transport us suddenly to the dedication of the temple. *See* the words of Solomon, 2 Chron. vi. 41, 42.

PSALM CXXXIII. Ver. 2. The blessings of unity are compared (1) to the holy oil which runs down to the skirts of the high priest's ("Aaron's") garments, and (2) to the moisture borne from the snow-capped Hermon, which falls by night in fertilizing small rain on the hills of Zion.

Ver. 3. *the night-mist*, a far more effectual refreshment than our "dew" to the parched earth during the summer of Palestine. Comp. *Korán*, ii. 267.

PSALM CXXXIV. From ver. 1 it has been thought that the officials who performed night service in the temple greeted each other in these words. Ver. 3 looks like a counter-greeting.

PSALM CXXXV. An admirable piece of mosaic-work, such as the devout students of Scripture after the Exile delighted in. Psalms, prophecies, and Pentateuch, have all contributed. Ver. 15-18 are borrowed from Ps. cxv. 4-8.

PSALM CXXXVI. A work in the same style. This psalm is generally called the great Hallel, though the Talmud also includes Ps. cxx.-cxxxv. under this title.

Ver. 25. *all flesh*, i.e. all living creatures, as Gen. vi. 13, 17, vii. 15.

PSALM CXXXVII. An ideal picture of national mourning. The actual experience of the exile was of course much more complex than the psalm would suggest. Hence this poem is probably a monument of the literary art of the post-Exile period. The feud between the Jews and the Edomites lasted till the final humiliation of the latter under John Hyrcanus. (Josephus, *Ant.* xiii. 9, 1.)

PSALM CXXXVIII. Ver. 2. *in the face of the gods*, i.e. the gods of the nations, who have been tried and found wanting by their worshippers. *thou hast magnified* . . . , i.e. thou hast given promises more glorious than the sun in the heavens. *Comp.* Ps. xix.

Ver. 6. The antithesis is not clearly expressed ; *afar off* requires to be balanced by "close at hand." There are two favourite spots with God—"the high and holy place," and "with him that is crushed and lowly in spirit" (Isa. lvii. 15). It requires self-humiliation to reach these crushed and lowly ones, *but the haughty He knows* (even) *afar off*.

Psalm CXXXIX. The most sublime of all the psalms, though one of the latest. The author revels in the thoughts of God's omniscience and omnipresence, and his one stumbling-block is the existence of the ungodly. The Christian reader will have to transform the last stanza!

Ver. 9. *If I lift up* . . . , i.e. if I could fly with the speed with which the dawn spreads over the sky. A myth weakened into a symbol. Comp. "the eyelids of the dawn," Job iii. 9, xli. 10. *the sea*, i.e. the western or Mediterranean sea.

Ver. 15. *in the underworld*. An enigmatical expression for the womb.

Ver. 16. *Mine unshapen mass*, i.e. the embryo. *they all*, viz. the appointed days.

Ver. 18. *I am still* (occupied) *with thee:* "still," because even my dreams hovered about the beloved theme. *Comp.* Cant. v. 2.

Psalm CXLI. A most obscure psalm; verses 5-7 seem hopeless in the present state of the text.

Psalm CXLIV. Another piece of post-Exile mosaic-work; *comp.* especially Ps. viii. xviii. Verses 12-15 are very original in style.

Ver. 12. *as cornices.* . . . Syrian architecture still delights in ornamenting corners of rooms with variegated carved work. Such corners may be figurative of the seclusion of an Eastern maiden.

Psalm CXLV. An alphabetic psalm, deficient, however, in the verse with *Nūn*.

Psalm CXLVI. The first of the joyous Hallelujah psalms. God's omnipotence, faithfulness, righteousness, and bounty.

Psalm CXLVII. Notice the immediateness of the relation of God to nature, and also the admiration expressed for the phenomena of a severe winter.

Psalm CXLIX. The duty of praise is here strangely supplemented by that of warring against the Gentiles. The "afflicted" and the "lovers of God" (loving ones) are the Jews of the Maccabean period, whose victories are described in heightened terms in ver. 7-9. With ver. 6 *comp.* 2 Macc. xv. 26, 27, "But Judas and his company encountered the enemies with invocation and prayer; so that fighting with their hands, and praying unto God with their hearts, they slew no less than thirty and five thousand men."

PSALM CL. is as evidently intended for the close, as Ps. 1 for the opening of a collection of psalms. The climax in ver. 6 is worthy of "The Book of Praises."

www.ingramcontent.com/pod-product-compliance
Lightning Source LLC
Chambersburg PA
CBHW032111230426
43672CB00009B/1704